Feather and Firesnake
The Maat of Kundalini

NEMA

BLACK MOON PUBLISHING
CINCINNATI, OHIO USA

Black Moon Manifesto

*It is the Will and mission of Bate Cabal/Black Moon to
effectively manifest unique and insightful occult Works
for the esoteric community in a manner that is unfettered
by commercial considerations.*

BlackMoonPublishing.com

blackmoonpublishing@gmail.com

Design and layout by
Jo Bounds of Black Moon

ISBN: 978-1-890399-74-0

United States • United Kingdom • Europe • Australia • India • Japan

CONTENTS

PREFACE

If the condition of the priesthood is a soul on fire with love (*The Priesthood*; Black Moon Publishing), then Nema is surely a priestess of the Word, a priestess of Truth, a priestess of Maat. The Feather and the Fire Snake is scribed from the wisdom and understandings of such a priestess. The fire is not to be found only in the belly of the snake but in the abysmal depths of the seeker's soul. At our core, as at the core of every star, is a heat that transforms all it touches. It is as a black flame that claims its own in passionate embrace. Some of the knowledge, some of the warmth, some of the heat of this fire radiates from Nema's text.

This is the fierce love (Zayin; bate cabal) of an awakening being. The publication does not invite reading or study so much as experience. Nema invites the soul of the reader to enter this fire and be consumed to rise again as a phoenix. In essence, reborn to Maat or truth.

This book is first and foremost about the wisdom gained through practice. As such, it evokes in the reader a desire and a commitment to practice. There is great value here in that practice brings the self of the practitioner into plain view. The possible pretenses of theory fall away easily in practice's crucible. Nema has placed the Feather and the Fire Snake on the pattens of Balance's scale and found a dynamic equilibrium that invites a committed active participation.

Pay special attention to Magick for Fools. It caries within it the kernel of a special understanding of the heart of the western majical system. Here one can travel on Nema's words and bring

back much of importance. To speak clearly and precisely about such a melange of difficult topics is both a difficult and an exciting undertaking.

Nema is a friend, a colleague, and was there from the very beginning of the cabals that emerged in Cincinnati. We share so much. It is an honor to be involved in the publishing of a work that allows Nema to share a part of the wonder that she is.

Louis Martinié
March, 2010v

FOREWORD

The Macedonian Lectures

In the early 1990s, my friend and colleague, Dr. Julijan Naskov of Macedonia, asked me to write a series of lectures for his proposed Academy of New Age Spiritual Sciences. He would have them translated into Serbo-Croatian and Albanian, and have them presented to his students by a lecturer of the Academy. Student responses, questions and comments would be translated into English for me, not only to answer as an immediate information-exchange, but also as raw material for a book to be written on the lectures.

We agreed that a good topic for intermediary or advanced students would be that of Kundalini and its application in Maat Magick.

Kundalini is the neurospiritual force associated with the human spinal cord and brain. Concentrations or nodes of this force are called Chakras. The major Chakras are aligned with and on the spinal cord and brain, and are activated as the Kundalini rises from the tailbone to the skull.

Magick is the art and the science of causing change to occur in conformity with Will. Maat Magick is concerned with individual self-transcendence, with assisting the human species to achieve its next stage of evolution, and in communication with non-human intelligence.

Information on the Chakras and on the Forgotten Ones is included in these lectures. "Forgotten Ones" is my term for

our survival instincts that seem to have a life of their own. I was pleased to note that the Forgotten Ones match up with the Chakras rather neatly.

I have heard from Mr. Viktor Radun, a colleague of Dr. Naskov, who has translated the lectures and has presented them in his city of Novi Sad.

On a tip from a friend, I suggest you record the guided meditations from the lectures, then play them back to help you travel along with them.

Awakening the powers of Kundalini is, in my opinion, a necessary Initiation on the path of High Magick. The forces of Magick are fierce and swift; the wise mage aligns and purifies all internal vessels and conduits, lest the winds of change and the fires of Will ignite imbalances and unresolved issues within him or her.

Understanding of our Forgotten Ones is also a necessary Initiation. When Magick is summoned for change, we must know ourselves well enough to ensure that the changes wrought within ourselves are the kind we need.

It has also occurred to me that the image of Kundalini as a vertical serpent can change into other shapes at need. In the cyclical changes of death and birth, as well as in the singular nature of eternity, the serpent bends to bite its own tail as Oroboros. In its destructive aspect, it swims the night horizontally as the serpent, Apep, who seeks to devour the sun god Ra, as the divine barque sails from west to east in the underworld.

I consider this book to be a group working, and I thank all involved for their interest and their time.

I hope the information here proves helpful to your Work.

Introductory Lecture

We all have one thing in common—an interest in Magick. I hope that you are presently practicing Magick, or intend to practice it in the near future. Just learning about Magick will not change you nor the world around you; Magick begins and ends in the physical world, although the middle parts happen in ways and in places that the uninitiated know little about.

When I use the word "Magick", I mean it in the sense of Aleister Crowley's definition: "Magick is the Science and the Art of causing change to occur in conformity with Will." Maat Magick is based on the concept of Maat, the Egyptian neter, or personification of truth, justice, honesty, accuracy and balance.

In Egyptian artwork, Maat is pictured as a beautiful young woman, daughter of Ra and wife of Tehuti/Thoth, who wears a feather in her headband. She is the measure against which the hearts of the dead are weighed in the scale of Anubis in the court of Osiris in the Hall of the Maati. Such a judgment scene is shown in the Papyrus of Ani in the British Museum.

Maat Magick is a form of Thelemic Magick, and fits into Crowley's scheme of Aeons. He based his theory of Aeons, or distinct periods of time when humanity thought and acted in certain ways, on the sacred Name of God, Tetragrammaton (YHVH), as represented by Egyptian godforms.

Yod (the Father) was a time of invasion, conquest, farming, and city-building, and had its image in Osiris. In the Western and Middle Eastern world, the Aeon of Osiris saw the rise of Judaism, Christianity, and Islam. Crowley saw the end of the Aeon of Osiris at the writing of the Book of the Law, Liber AL vel Legis.

He' (the Mother) had her time before the Aeon of Osiris, even though her letter comes second in Tetragrammaton. The Aeon of Isis was a time of nomadic tribes, when the Goddess was venerated as the Earth, and as nature, under different names in different places. Her Aeon saw the changes of humanity from hunter to herdsman to farmer to citizen.

Vau (the Son) is Horus, the hawk-headed Lord of the Sun, and child of Isis and Osiris. According to Crowley, the Aeon of Horus began in 1904 with the writing of the Book of the Law, and continues to this day. The task of this Aeon is to destroy the remains of the Aeon of Osiris, to wipe out all the institutions of repression—bad government, bad schools, bad churches, slavery and wars, and all situations where one person tries to control the thoughts and actions of another person.

Second He' (the Daughter), is Maat, whose Aeon began in 1974 e.v. with the writing of *Liber Pennae Praenumbra*. The Aeon of Maat did not end the Aeon of Horus, but is in effect along with it. Maat's work is to rebuild a new world society from the ashes of the Osirian Aeon, making sure that justice and truth are given a chance to guide human life, everywhere.

This sounds like an impossible job, but if our Magick is done well and done correctly, we can do it.

I've added two more Aeons to Crowley's original four. Bes, the dwarf god from the interior of Africa, represents the Nameless Aeon, the times of prehistory before the Aeon of Isis. He represents the Ancestors, the shamans, the first humans to watch the stars and the world around them and to do rituals and trances to heal, hunt, and speak with the spirits.

Harpocrat, the child seated on a lotus or standing on a

crocodile, is the Lord of Silence and the image for the Wordless Aeon, the times of the future. He signifies the Descendants, our children and grandchildren and their children.

The nature of Magick itself has evolved through the Aeons, since each Aeon has its own Magickal Formula and change in the direction of the Magickal Current. The late Twentieth and early Twenty-first Centuries comprise a time of major world change, and seems to many people to be chaotic, dangerous and threatening. Discoveries in science and technology are occurring too often to allow for even one generation to pass before reality shifts into a new mode. We've gone from the first flight of the Wright brothers' airplane at Kitty Hawk to walking on the moon in less than a century. I can still remember a time without television, and now there is a globe-spanning computer Internet, communications satellites, and cell phones. Even though some people feel lost and fearful, it's a wonderful time to be alive.

This chaotic time of transition is excellent for Magick. Nothing is nailed down tight, except for the absolute fact that tomorrow won't be like today. We have the opportunity to create a more effective manner of changing ourselves and the world.

The ancient High Magick of the Aeon of Bes we know little about, except that neatly-placed bear skulls in a cave seem to indicate that the bear was either worshipped as a supernatural being, or was seen as a way into power for the tribe. At some burial sites, red ocher on human bones seems to show that the ancestors believed in some type of life after death.

Most of what we know of prehistoric Magick is guesswork, but practices of primitive tribes today may give us clues to the ways of the past. It's also helpful to travel to the Inner planes to imagine (or remember) what your own Magick would be like if you lived under the same conditions that our earliest human ancestors did.

When our brains became complex enough to house a mind complex enough to have abstract thoughts, and to form language refined enough to discuss abstractions, we began to try to make

sense of the world around us and to understand the meaning of life. For the forces beyond our control, such as weather, sexual desire, fertility of the tribe and of the food supply, death, dreams, and so on, we invented personalities and called them gods and spirits. We drew parallels and comparisons between them and our own emotions and experiences, and so came to picture the gods and spirits as human-like with (at times) animal characteristics that signified specific powers. Like humans, the gods were male and female (with an occasional androgyne), and the roles assigned them reflected their gender characteristics.

We assumed that the gods and spirits could be influenced, as human beings are influenced, by gifts and praise or by approved behavior. If flattery and praise worked on those humans who were bigger and stronger than we were, and who could be bribed into not hurting us, then the gods and spirits should be able to be influenced and bribed in the same way. Thus began religious worship and sacrifice. Beyond the avoidance of pain, religion began to be seen as a source of blessing also, if our gifts and behavior were acceptable and pleasing.

The gods and spirits developed as our experiences developed, changing to meet the public and private needs of humans.

The Aeon of Isis brought the transition from hunting and herding to the development of agriculture, cities, and the art of writing. The image of the Goddess changed from crude figurines and drawings of the All-Mother to a multitude of personalities and patronage of love, war, seasonal changes and aspects of Nature. Ishtar/Astarte/Ashtoreth was strong, desirable, fierce, beautiful and powerful. Mystery schools and bodies of Initiates, such as those of the Eleusinian Mysteries, formed around the mystical aspects of the natural world, seeing death and rebirth mirrored in the turning of the seasons and in the myth of Demeter and Persephone. In Egypt, priesthoods and Temples of the various neter/gods discovered the Magick of the Word, of the powers of Names, of the value of writing.

In the Aeon of Isis, Magick became intricate and specialized;

it began to distinguish itself from religion in a number of ways. The essential feature of Magick is that it works by command instead of prayer. The idea is that if you know the True Name of an entity, you can bind it to your Will, since a True Name is the essence of a thing's nature. Another tool for working Magick is the Word of Power, to be spoken in one's True Voice, or "Ma Kheru". The Ma Kheru is discovered through self-knowledge, and is seated in the core of one's being. Speaking with it creates vibrations that speed through the world and change the object of the Magickal intention.

Isis was considered to be such a great Magickian that she was able to gain control over Ra himself by forcing him to reveal his True Name to her. She caused a venomous serpent to bite the Sun God and bring him near death, then withheld the antidote to the poison until he told her his True Name. There are still cultures alive today where you keep your True Name a secret so that none may gain power over you.

The Aeon of Osiris gradually dawned when population pressures required tribes and nations to move beyond former territories whose land, animals and plants could no longer support them. When these traveling tribes met the natives of the lands they found, wars of conquest and defense often determined who controlled the disputed territory. Male gods, gods of war and kingship, gods of a fatherhood that held the power of life and death over wives and children, soon overshadowed and obscured the worship of the goddess, the reverence of the Maiden, the Mother, and the Crone.

The father-gods were the Lords of High Places, such as the Aryan sky-gods, Indra and Varuna, Daius Pitar/Zeus/Jupiter of the Mediterranean region, or Yahveh meeting his prophets on the mountaintops. The goddesses had been of the earth, moon and stars, but the gods were of the storms, the thunder and lightning. As seems to be human custom, the gods of the conquered peoples became the demons of the conquerors, and the ideals of the warrior son and the ruling father found expression in the

absolute authority of the male over female.

The height of the Aeon of Osiris expressed itself in Judaism, Christianity and Islam; in the medieval centuries, the beginnings of secular science separated from Magick in Alchemy and Qaballah. The latter gave rise to mathematics and theology, and the former to chemistry. Astronomy has even older roots, as astrology reaches back into prehistory.

Magick, in the Aeon of Osiris, operated on the formula of the Dying God, with a rebirth or resurrection completing the Mystery of death. Magick reached toward the Outer, physical world, as evidenced by the alchemical goals of the Philosophers' Stone and the Elixir of Life. The Stone of the Wise was supposed to be able to turn base metals into gold, and the Elixir was reputed to impart youth and immortality. Enquiry into the physical realm was tolerated by the established religions, while the spiritual realm became the exclusive property of the church, synagogue and mosque.

The nearest thing to traffic with spirits and demons were spells and conjurations using various names of God to compel the unseen entities to serve the Magickian's will; the thin tolerance of such practices by the Church depended on maintaining the formality of God's supremacy in all operations. I interpret the legend of Faust as Church propaganda warning of the dangers of lust for knowledge; far better to be a sheep fed on faith than a dupe of the Devil.

Followers of the Old Religions were condemned as witches by the Inquisition, and were accused of worshipping Satan—even though Satan, as a fallen angel and enemy of God, was a Christian invention.

The greatest contribution of the Osirian Aeon to the practice of Magick was the invention of the scientific method, the use of experimentation and research. The outstanding example of Magickal experimentation during this Aeon would be the work of John Dee and Edward Kelly in their scrying which yielded the Enochian/Angelic language. At the transition of the Magickal

Current from the Aeon of Osiris to the Aeon of Horus, Aleister Crowley also put much emphasis on the scientific method.

In the Aeon of Horus, the concept of True Will (Thelema) seems to be the core contribution to the High Art. The decay of the Osirian Current had brought Magick to the sorry state of repeating itself fruitlessly, manifesting in fossilized Lodge rituals, in spiritualistic seances of doubtful honesty and in cosmic scenarios of Root Races and Perfect Masters. In the search for True Will, however, the Initiate had to do genuine work on the Inner planes to acquire self-knowledge. Traditional rites and practices were of minimum help, warming-up exercises only.

Thelema, as a system of Magick, reaches beyond the cramped and petty aims of a search for gold and eternal youth, and adopts Oriental wisdom; True Will is indistinguishable from the Tao. Crowley was also a great syncretist, traveling around the world and collecting theories and practices from many cultures; these he incorporated into his system to the benefit of us who are his Magickal heirs. He also brought women and the goddess back into the temple, although in ways adjusted to his liking and always in partnership with a male entity. Nuit had her Hadit, Babalon her Pan, and the Scarlet Woman is ever with her Beast.

Horus enthroned Osiris in the Kingdom of the Dead and became the Lord of the Living. The Magickal task of the Aeon of Horus is the destruction of the remnants of the Aeon of Osiris. Many of our traditional institutions, such as Church, State, national boundaries, xenophobic tribalism and domestic despotism have outlived their survival value and are hampering human development. The enlightened anarchy that would replace these institutions can only function when everyone knows his or her True Will and practices it.

The Aeon of Maat is running concurrently with the Aeon of Horus. We don't exist in a vacuum, and if Horus is busy destroying the poisons and restrictions of the past, Maat is working to change the human race into a species that doesn't need what is disintegrating.

If you use the ideas and power of the Maat Current correctly, you become a living talisman of our species, a pioneer whose explorations unlock a new way of being and living. As you deliberately undertake the mutation into double consciousness, you broadcast information of your experiences and methods into the astral menstruum/Akasha from which other seekers and changers can receive it, modify it, and use it in the ways most suited to individual circumstances. You also write about it and speak about it in situations where it's appropriate to do so.

As the Daughter of Tetragrammaton, Maat is not merely an echo of the Mother. She is a new force, acting above the relevance of gender, free of dependency on relationships even though her "specialty" is the formation and change of all types of relationships. She needs no male to validate her or her power and principles, nor does she need another female; she herself is both and neither.

The Magick of Maat transcends the aims of past Magicks. Although Maat Magick can manifest as humbly as the sharing of a cup of a healing herbal tea, it cares nothing for the transmutation of metals or for finding eternal life. Even though Maat Magick has several forms of banishment and exorcism, it marches into the dark side of existence to investigate and control the monsters of the Inner and the Outer worlds. If any of the traditional benefits of Magick—such as wealth, influence, fame, longevity, command of Elementals, demons, angels, devas or the invoking of gods and the gaining of their power—come into the possession of a Maat Magickian, they are merely unimportant side effects of the main aim.

The aim of Maat Magick is threefold: a) the personal transformation of the Maat Magickian through deep self-knowledge into a double-consciousnessed Homo veritas and unit of Divine Intelligence; b) the transformation of the human race, through the conscious work of the living and of the soon-to-be-born, into Homo veritas, the new species of mankind; and c) educating ourselves into a mind large enough to successfully

communicate and act with nonhuman intelligences. The Magicks of the Wordless Aeon are beyond the scope of these lectures. When you become adept at Maat Magick, their nature will present itself to you.

I'm sure that you can think of many more details, confirmations and contradictions to the sketchy history of Magick presented here. I have a few points to think about and perhaps to discuss among yourselves.

• Why should anyone study and practice Magick?

• What are your purposes in life, beyond the basic biological urges?

• What can Magick do for you that you couldn't get from science, art, religion or philosophy?

• What is your opinion about God; telepathy; existence after death; Jesus Christ; Javeh; Allah; Buddha; human evolution; science; art; UFO's and aliens?

• What is your vision of your own future, and of the future of the human race?

Your answers will tell you much about yourself and about the direction your practices will take you.

LECTURE 2

lthough many people begin studying Magick for limited or nebulous reasons such as fame and fortune or curiosity about the Occult, Magick's primary effect is the personal transformation of the Magickian. For the noble of heart who see the sorry condition of the world today and want to change it for the better, the idea of personal transformation may seem too self-centered and too narrow. The Maat, the Truth of the situation is: unless we become fully human, unless we shape ourselves, our talents and our power into a clean and concentrated instrument, we lack the means to change the world.

So how do we begin the Great Work of transformation? We review what we know about ourselves before moving on to discover that which we don't know. Our busy lives leave little time for examining ourselves, hardly a chance for contemplation and meditation on our Inner realities. We have to make time for this; openings between obligations and events will not occur spontaneously, so they must be manufactured. We need to secure at least an hour a day for our Magick at a time when we aren't too tired or sleepy to maintain full alertness and attention.

We also need to make a place in which to do Magick, a special sacred space dedicated to the Work, a Temple. Most of us live in cities, towns or villages where the privacy and solitude of the woods, shore or mountain are not available to us on a

daily basis. We must then plan on using an indoor space for our Temple. Use your creativity and ingenuity in this. If you don't have the luxury of a regular room that you can use exclusively as a Temple, then seek out an attic, basement, garage, stable, etc. that can be converted by Art and Will into your holy ground. If necessary, use a room dedicated to other purposes, a room that you can change into your Temple by moving the furniture around, lighting candles and incense, turning off the lights and banishing thoroughly.

Find or make the classical Magickal tools of wand, sword, cup and pentacle as you locate a table or other surface to use as an altar. An appropriate cloth to drape over it can make an altar from a desk, a packing crate or a chair. Let your sense of Art range freely. Get a notebook to use for your Magickal Record, and write in it every day. When you have your Temple and its furnishings and tools assembled, create a ritual for dedicating it and them to the Great Work and to the Maat, the truth of your essential self.

A physical Temple of some kind, no matter how sketchy and symbolic you make it, is necessary to Magick, and especially Maat Magick, since your Work must engage your whole self in order to succeed. Never fall into the trap of "working only on the Astral". A "library Magickian" is only an intellectual dilettante who denies himself or herself the full experience of the Magickal process. Those who disdain the physical world are trapped in a wrong idea and will remain impotent to change anything.

It's been traditional among Mystics and Seekers to "renounce the world" in order to devote all one's time to the pursuit of spiritual truth, but truth can be found "in the world" as well as in a separation from it. The key to balancing making a living and interacting among family and friends with Magickal/Mystical work is to practice living in the point of view that everything is sacred, everything is alive, and everything has something to teach us.

One of the more valuable concepts Western Magick has

learned from the East is that of the Chakras and Kundalini. The Chakras are points of concentrated energy in the human nervous system; the ones we will be considering for our structure in these lectures are the eight major Chakras aligned along our spine. The imagery of lotus flowers and spinning circles of light are useful for visualizing the Chakras and for concentrating the attention upon each one. Kundalini is an energizing force that lies coiled at the base of the spine, a force that rises from one Chakra to the next.

The lower Chakras are at least partly activated with Kundalini by our natural biological processes, and Kundalini can rise spontaneously to levels not prepared for its presence. Part of the Magickian's self-knowledge includes familiarity with and control of our physical-Astral energy systems. The traditional image of Kundalini is that of a fiery serpent coiled three and a half times around the Shivalingam, which is the root of existence.

Maat Magick deals with the Forgotten Ones, our survival urges that we need to control and use as sources of our personal Magickal power. The Forgotten Ones link with the Chakras directly, and it seems to be a linkage useful to our purposes here.

We begin with three basic elements: the physical universe with our Temples in it; the Muladhara Chakra at the anus-perineum; the Forgotten One of Hunger. I say "Temples" in the plural because our own physical body is our first Temple; the one we build to work in is an extension of our body.

The physical universe as we know it is the product of the interaction of great spiritual forces and is made of the density of energy holding to temporarily stable configurations. Our physical bodies participate in the general nature of the universe, since they are composed of particles, atoms, molecules, cells, tissues and organs, all of which are arrangements of energy in a Universal Pattern of Consciousness.

This Universal Pattern of Consciousness is echoed throughout the planes of existence with variations and elaborations, in the Astral realms of dreams and instincts, and in the worlds of mind,

emotions, self-awareness, intuition and spirit. There is a Divine Intelligence that informs all of existence, from subatomic particles to galaxies. One of the sayings of Maat Magick is: All that is, lives; all that lives is intelligent. The more complex the entity, the more comprehensive and sophisticated is the intelligence it has. The visions of Maat Magick reveal that Homo sapiens is presently in the mid-range of complexity and intelligence, and stands ready to change into a new level with the emergence of the Racial Unconscious of Jung into a species consciousness.

As Magickians, we employ the Universal Pattern of Consciousness to transfer our progress and attainments to our species as a whole; thus, we function as living talismans of the human race. Our responsibilities are not just to ourselves, but to everyone. We begin the fulfillment of our mission with the establishment of our body's well-being and of our Temple's existence and dedication. This readies us for our own Magickal work and lays the foundations of our Magickal Link with the rest of humanity.

Whenever you do a Magickal ritual, or meditate, in your Temple or elsewhere, perform a banishment of your immediate environment in order to clear it of negative influences or energy that might interfere with the success of your work. For the banishment to work on you also, cast off any thoughts or feelings that would harm the work. This would include anger, worry, depression, envy, hatred and fear, or any thoughts of problems in your life.

A standard Magickal banishment, the Lesser Ritual of the Pentagram, can be found in Liber O vel Manus et Sagittae by Aleister Crowley. Maat Magick has two major banishments, the Eight-fold and the Six-fold.

In the Eight-fold banishment, stand facing South, trace an "S" in the air before you and say, "Shaitan"; at the South-East put your right index finger to your lips and say, "Heru Pa Kraat"; at the East, take one step forward with your right foot, arms extended before you with palms facing forward, saying,

"Ra Hoor Khuit"; step back, then face the North-East, touch your forehead with your right forefinger and say, "Hadit". At the North, trace an arch in the air from left to right with your right hand and say, "Nuit"; at the North-West, place your flat left hand horizontally on top of your vertical, flat right hand and say, "Maat"; at the West, form both hands into cups and say, "Babalon"; at the South-West, extend the index fingers and small fingers of both hands above your head, then bend to touch them to the ground as you say, "Aiwass". At the end of your main work, close by performing the banishment in reverse.

In the Six-fold banishment, begin by calling down into the earth, "Bes! Ancestor of us all! Guard this sacred space." Assume his godform until you feel his essence enter you like strong old roots anchoring you to the earth. The godform of Bes is that of a dwarf from the African interior. Point your knees outward and bend them until your thighs are horizontal, while your upper arms are also horizontal and out to the side; your lower arms are held upright and your hands are fists; your tongue protrudes slightly.

Facing South, you call, "Osiris! Father of us all! Guard this sacred space." Assume his godform by crossing your arms on your chest, imagining that you hold the crook and flail of the Pharaohs. Hold the gesture until you feel the force of fire and will enter you.

At the West, call, "Isis! Mother of us all! Guard this sacred space." Assume her godform by cradling your left arm as though holding an infant, and position your right hand as though guiding the infant to your breast. Maintain her posture until you are filled with the power of water and love.

At the East, call, "Horus! Elder Brother of us all! Guard this sacred space." Place your left hand in a fist over your heart and raise your right fist with your shoulder bent at 90 degrees to your body and your elbow bent 90 degrees from your upper arm. Hold this godform until you feel the invisible strength of the winds and the clarity of still air suffuse your mind.

At the North, call, "Maat! Elder Sister of us all! Guard this sacred space." Take her godform by placing your flat left hand horizontally atop your flat, vertical right hand. Hold the position until you feel the solidity of earth and the dance of the atoms at the same time.

Looking directly overhead, call, "Harpocrat! Descendant of us all! Guard this sacred space." Assume his godform by placing your right index finger, or your right thumb to your lips. Hold this gesture until your entire being is flooded with silence and joy.

At the end of your work, reverse the order of the names and draw the essences of all the godforms into yourself.

The room is as psychically clear as it can be. Sit comfortably and close your eyes. Visualize your consciousness as a point of light about 4 centimeters behind your eyes and about 6 centimeters down from the roof of your skull. This is where you usually live during your ordinary waking life, but you don't have to stay there.

Move yourself to the back of your brain, illuminating the neurons and the structures they form by the light you radiate. Move downward from your cerebrum to your cerebellum, down your brainstem to your spinal cord, down the length of the cord to its end in your coccyx. Ride your long, white, gleaming bundle of nerve tissue; note its branchings on either side through each vertebra. When you reach the end of the cord in its final nexus, use your astral vision to see through bone, muscle, blood vessels, skin and clothing; look around the room from your new, lower vantage point.

Turn your astral senses back inward and focus on your anus, on the powerful muscles of the sphincter, on the glowing sphere of energy there, spinning slowly and unfolding itself like the petals of a lotus. This is the Muladhara Chakra, home of Kundalini the Fire Snake.

This is the part of the body held in lowest esteem, and yet how beautiful is its power and structure! It is the end of the

alimentary canal that begins at the mouth, the exit for the food we've eaten after our body has extracted the energy-producing molecules from it and reclaimed a good percentage of its water content. It's the exit also for the chemicals our body makes for digesting our food, chemicals from our stomach, liver, pancreas and the lining of our intestines. It's the gate of purification for our own dead cells and spent secretions, the means by which we empty ourselves to make room for fresh food and new energy.

When you have a clear picture of this shrine at the base of your spine, slowly bring the point of your consciousness back up your spine to your brain, letting it settle back into its usual place behind your eyes.

On a more spiritual level, the Muladhara Chakra is our lower gate of retention and release of Magical power; it keeps us from becoming Black Brothers (not a racial term) in the Abyss. As a model of how Magick works, think of the Magickal Current as a powerful river. The Magickian is a tube, or hose, that immerses its upper end in the flow and directs the volume of the water it can divert into, and through, itself at situations needing to be changed. Black Brothers are those who want to contain the Current in themselves, to hold the power coming into them without letting it go to benefit the world. They think that hoarding Magickal power will increase their own personal power, giving them control over other people, making themselves feared, respected and obeyed.

The Magickal Current is too strong for anyone to hold or contain it, of course, so those who seal off the Muladhara, who clamp down on the outflow of the Current, swell up and burst on the astral planes, leaving their shredded remains to be washed away. The Black Brothers who fear this happening try to avoid it by sealing off their upper ends as well as their lower ends, thus cutting themselves out of the flow of the Current entirely. These people then shrivel and shrink away to a dried husk. The only way to use Magick safely is to be an open tube, directing power by Will and being nourished and strengthened by it in

the process.

Nourishment is the oldest need of living things; the animal instinct is to find food and eat it when we are hungry. The plant instinct is to convert sunlight, carbon dioxide and water into sugars and starches, spreading the growth of root and leaf in the process. The crystal instinct is to attract to itself the atoms and molecules of its structure from its environment, aligning them in orderly growth.

In the Animal Kingdom, hunger is far older an instinct than sex. Even single cell animals seek out food, surround it and absorb it. In our civilized times, in normal circumstances, food is available for the purchase all year around; most humans alive today no longer rely on the uncertain luck of the hunt or the uncertain abundance or scarcity of wild plants in order to get their food. Except for conditions of war or of extreme poverty, we have forgotten the force of physical hunger, the power that hunger exerts over our actions.

Hunger, in its fulfillment, insures the continued living of the individual organism, providing fuel for action and materials for tissue growth and repair. This fact is so common and obvious that we forget that it's a survival urge, a basic set of sensations and responses that have kept us alive and evolving from the first cells in ancient oceans to the complexity of our present lives.

So how do we use this urge, this Forgotten One, of hunger? Ancient mystics of all cultures knew the value of fasting to clarify the mind and to gain spiritual power. To craft a ritual for the purpose of bringing this oldest Forgotten One to the full light of consciousness and uniting with it, plan several periods of fasting before the rite. During this preparation time, contemplate the mechanisms and sensations of hunger. Consider also the nature of the Muladhara Chakra as the home of Kundalini and of the nearness of the anus to the earth and its organic life.

Think about our design as a hollow tube, the inside of which is almost four times longer than its outside. Think about the anus as the final part of the inside labyrinth that begins with

the mouth, as the controlled seal that, together with the mouth, makes us an open or a closed system.

For the ritual itself, obtain your favorite food and have it on your altar as a sacrifice. Plan the ritual to be at the end of a twenty-four hour fast. Be sure to drink plenty of liquids as you abstain from food, and get as much rest as possible. The actual ritual itself I leave to your own creative abilities. It is a good idea to make certain practices, such as banishing, scribing the circle, setting up the Watchtowers of the elements and cardinal directions, etc. part of your normal ritual custom. I also suggest that you build the energies slowly to an irresistible climax, and take enough time in ending the rite after you've eaten the food to make note of the sensations of hunger satisfied.

It's important to record your plans and preparations, as well as the ritual itself, in your Magickal Record. Write down what actually happened in the ritual, what you aimed to accomplish by doing it, and to what degree the ritual succeeded. Include any difficulties you may have had, before, during, or after the rite. What thoughts and feelings did you experience?

To review: In this session, we have discussed the lowermost Chakra, the Muladhara. We see how important it is for Magick (and the Magickian) to be well-Earthed, in terms of establishing a Temple, in knowing how to banish it and in using it to do ritual. We have taken an astral journey inside our bodies to become aware of the home of Kundalini, and we have spoken of the Forgotten One of hunger. We have also mentioned the idea of the Magickian as a hollow tube—like the hollow tube in which Prometheus brought the fire of the gods to humanity— and the ways in which the anus and the Muladhara Chakra keep us open to the Cosmos and the Magickal Current.

As an exercise for the first Chakra, establish your sacred space, your temple, and furnish it according to the direction of your imagination and spirit. If you already have a temple, draw a picture of it, or attach a photo of it, in your Magickal Record.

Be aware of the food you eat, and of its stately progress

through your body. Make a donation to a local food pantry for the poor.

LECTURE 3

At our last meeting, we discussed the basics of practical Magick: setting up our physical Temples and Altars, acquiring our Magickal tools, making a habit of banishing before and after rituals and other Temple Work, and becoming familiar with the idea of Kundalini and our lowest Chakra. All this activity is like establishing oneself as an adult economically and socially; the basic needs of survival have been taken care of, and now it's time to explore other facets of life and Magick.

It should be no surprise that the first topic to arise, after one's individual well-being has been dealt with, is sex. Did the interest level in the room suddenly become more intense? Let's raise it further. Sex and sexuality are vital Magickal tools as well as sources of power. Sex is not to be repressed and denied. Sexuality is not dirty nor shameful; it is our species' means of continued existence and it is the individual's gateway into life.

Why then, has Christian tradition treated sexuality as a shameful sin, something to be denied? Why have ascetics from other cultures recommended abstaining from sexual activity? In the first case, Christian spiritual writers say that human desire should be for union with God, not for union with other human beings. Some say that the Biblical story of Adam and Eve was a story of sexual indulgence as the Original Sin, that the "forbidden fruit" was the ecstasy of sexual intercourse. Even the Sacrament of Marriage is held to be a poor second choice to virginity and

chastity. As Saint Paul remarks, "It is better to marry than to burn."

There are people who hold that matter is evil and spirit is good. Everything that increases the realm of matter, and especially that which combines matter with spirit (as is the case with human beings) is hateful. Having babies is bringing more evil into the world, such people would say; sex is designed for making babies, therefore sex is evil. Nonreproductive sexual activity is also frowned upon, since those who hate matter often hate pleasure obtained through material means.

NonChristian ascetics seem to counsel sublimation, the conversion of the power of sex into spiritual power by not permitting sexuality its physical outlets. They hold that sexual activity depletes one's energy, weakens one, coarsens the intelligence and distracts focus away from spiritual practices and attitudes. There is a certain amount of truth in the idea of sublimation, but if you consider the effort, difficulty and time consumed in this method, it appears to be somewhat inefficient.

Maat Magick uses a simpler, more direct approach in putting the energies of sex to use in the service of the Great Work: understand your human nature, understand your sexual nature, and shape your rituals accordingly.

Observation of Nature, including us humans, is the first source of knowledge, understanding and wisdom. When we look at sex with the eyes of a child, that is, with no moral or philosophical agenda, we see that it is the way our species continues through time in a very long life. Individual humans live for a relatively short time, but they make babies with sex, they nurture and teach their children, passing on not only genetic information but also knowledge and culture.

Here is a useful mental tool for thinking about sex: each species of vegetable, animal and borderline life has a Deva, or spirit of its own, a spirit who is the essence of its species, who looks after the well-being of its species. The Deva is the particular genetic pattern of a species, the personality, as it were,

of the godhood of DNA. DNA is a practical, hands-on type of divinity, since it determines everything about our physical, emotional, and mental abilities.

From a Deva's point of view, individuals come into existence on the physical plane in order to permit DNA to combine its variations in constant patterns of change within the Genus. Many Genera have more than one species in physical existence; humanity thinks it only has one. Homo neanderthalensis is considered extinct, even though many of its traits manifest in H. sapiens. Homo veritas is beginning to manifest within the ranks of H. sapiens, even though we remain invisible.

The Deva of H. sapiens is a fearful and reluctant parent, even as it has been a fearful and reluctant sibling. H. sapiens murdered H. Neanderthalis as surely as Cain slew Abel. H. sapiens would murder H. veritas , if given the chance. Witness history, witness the daily news. Humans tend to define humanity as narrowly as possible while in their uninitiated, unawakened state. Xenophobia manifests among differing ethnic groups, nations, religions, clans, economic classes, castes, gender orientations, gangs and families. The Deva of H. sapiens is schizophrenic.

Even so, the crazy Deva is giving birth to a child who is eminently sane, whole, balanced and healthy. As I mentioned in the introductory lecture, the second major aim of Maat Magick is to assist in the emergence of a new human species, Homo veritas , people who are connected to each other consciously. This is such a simple, logical, obvious condition, once it's seen, absorbed and recognized!

In case you're wondering what all this has to do with sex, it has everything to do with sex. Sex is the second oldest Forgotten One, and is sometimes more powerful than Hunger or any of the other survival-urges. Even though sex runs more of our lives than we're usually willing to admit, there are "Forgotten" aspects of it that we need to understand and master so we can employ it correctly in our Magick.

DNA has manufactured us for sex, as amusing vehicles for its

own propagation, change and entertainment. Whether or not the human genetic spiral is capable of intention, satisfaction, humor or other attributes of complex intelligence, it is compelling, dictatorial and motivational in our views of life, our actions and our decisions. This doesn't seem to be a problem for our animal cousins; they follow instinct and generally live well.

Our problems with sex began with the emergence of Mind from our neural complexity, and with the development of self-distinction, or Ego, from Mind. The straightforward process of mate, make babies, raise babies to the state of independent survival, then die became complicated with factors of social status, territory, possessions and control over other individuals. The taboos, institutions and restrictions that arose around the urge to mate freely served only to distort and twist the expressions of that urge in many instances.

Maat Magick doesn't propose to restore its pristine innocence to our Forgotten One of sex; we deal with our resources as we find them. Sexual activity is the occasion when we are in the most direct contact with our DNA and its crazy Deva, so we adapt our approach to their obsessions. Our methods are not to release sexual energy for Magickal direction in the most direct or open way, but rather to generate a charge through the most elaborate labyrinths possible. The narrower the aperture, the more forceful the stream.

The most important fact about Sex Magick in general applies to Maatian Sex Magick: the release of orgasmic energy creates a Child on at least one of the planes of existence, whether that creation is Willed or otherwise. This applies to eighth degree (autoeroticism), ninth degree (heterosexual coupling), eleventh degree AC or eleventh degree KG. Aleister Crowley named the eleventh degree as homosexual coupling, and Kenneth Grant holds that the eleventh degree indicates heterosexual coupling during menstruation. All other sexual activity, with a few exceptions, can be seen as elaborations on the eighth degree.

The point here is the creation of a Magickal Child. Each

sexual act should be dedicated to a specific end, to a particular change you Will to make. Undirected Children will accumulate on the lower Astral planes, joining other incomplete and hungry entities who hover there, looking to draw on the life energy of the unaware. In ideal circumstances, a Magickian should make a ritual occasion of every orgasm. In practice, it's well to have a clear formulation of your Great Work, so that you can dedicate to it all instances of unexpected orgasm.

There are several aspects of Sex Magick, and the major ones employed in Maat Magick are as follows:

The manifestation of Will on the material plane, the astral plane, the mental plane etc. This is most efficiently done by creating a sigil of your desire, forgetting it, building a charge of the greatest possible intensity by refraining from the release of sexual tension, then releasing that tension in orgasm while visualizing the sigil, sending all the energy of the release into its form. It's possible to use various symbols of your intent as a sigil—Tarot cards, chess figures, candles, photographs, drawings, etc.

One of the most effective ways of creating a sigil is the method created by Austin Osman Spare. Write your desire in a sentence, then cross out each letter that appears a second time or more often. Take the remaining letters and use them to construct an abstract figure by reversing them, inverting them, fusing parts of them with other letters and so on. To complete the Working, use the sexual fluids to anoint the symbol of intent, and, if appropriate, destroy the symbol.

A second type of Sex Magick is that used for realization of consciousness in new ways through the temporary destruction of self-awareness in the state of ecstasy. Building a charge is useful here also. In the act itself, using a silent mantram or chant helps to peel away the connection of mind and "outside" observation of oneself or one's surroundings. Connect the rhythm of the repetitions of the word or words to the rhythm of the physical movements. It's important to fix your attention on the mantram

or chant rather than on your physical sensations, even though you are keenly aware of those sensations; continue the repetitions until you fall across the brink of the orgasmic cascade, at which point there is no "you" there to repeat anything.

Maintain this condition for as long as possible by remaining still and silent and keeping your breathing regular as it slows. Bring your body slowly back to waking consciousness, allowing the remnants of the "nothingness" to dissolve into your sense perceptions. Keep your mind in the world of sense perception for as long as possible, eating lightly and drinking herb tea in order to earth yourself. Bring whatever topics that are important to you before your mind, one at a time, contemplating them without analysis, criticism or judgment. Banish the Temple thoroughly before allowing the normal flow of mundane thinking and action to resume.

A third approach to using sex in Maat Magick is that of pleasure sacrifice in the invocation of a godform. In the course of your Initiations, you should include a period of experience in Bhakti Yoga, or devotional exercises. This is best done during your activation of the Heart Chakra, as you develop your ability to love under Will.

I refer you to Aleister Crowley's Liber Astarte vel Berylli for a thorough treatment of the matter, but the essence of the Maatian approach is to call your god or goddess into your body as you offer him/her/it the experience of your orgasm. This is more appropriate for some godforms than it is for others, of course. If your selected deity is of the Martial kind, you would probably choose an offering of belligerence or destruction rather than orgasm; if it's more Saturnian, you might flavor your orgasmic offering with bondage, and so on. Use your understanding of the nature of the various gods to tailor the form of the pleasure you offer them.

A fourth use is the induction of a channeling trance state through sexual arousal combined with other methods such as drumming, chanting, dancing, etc., which are used

as preliminaries to the sexual phase. Now in experimenting with these various methods, I strongly urge you to keep your activities to eighth degree work at first. The channeling trance is difficult to induce by yourself, but it can work with appropriate technology—especially that of a recording device.

Your Temple setup is especially important in this kind of Working; use whatever you have of candles, incense, fabrics of rich texture and smoothness, pictures and other images, wine, cakes and fruit, etc. You can call specific entities for communication, or you can address the Cosmos at large or your own Angel for information you need to have. In the early stages of such a rite, record yourself drumming and chanting for as long a period as seems right to you. Play back these sounds as you dance and sway until you reach a suspension of ordinary consciousness; that is, until your awareness is totally involved in your senses instead of in thought.

Change the recorder from "play" to "record", and proceed with the most subtle and delicate self-stimulation. Give voice to your feelings as you will; incoherent sounds will begin to form themselves into words as your identity becomes more and more absorbed in the sensations of pleasure. Come as close as you can to the brink of orgasm, repeatedly, without actually crossing over that brink. Let the voice or voices you hear from your own mouth speak for as long as they wish in whatever ways that they wish. Don't concern yourself with meanings or definitions during the process, no matter what strange words are spoken. The time for analysis is after the rite is completed.

When the message or messages are complete, a peculiar fatigue and lassitude should overcome you, despite any residual arousal that remains from your stimulations. Allow yourself to rest or sleep at this point; any hazard from candles should have been seen to before the ritual began, so that you are free from worry at the end. When you wake, close the rite, banish the Temple and gently earth yourself with food and drink.

A fifth type of Maatian Sex Magick is Astral congress with

nonhuman entities. The aim of this type of Working is to expand your views of reality and to open yourself to a larger sense of kinship with all manifestations of Intelligence. In Nature, the little god DNA separates the species by cross-infertility. Some hybrids are possible, like mules and tiglons/ligers (the offspring of lions and tigers), but the hybrids themselves are usually sterile. In the realm of Magick and Mysticism, the Magickal Children of wildly divergent life-forms can be fertile and potent generators of change.

I would like to note at this point that some Magickal Children are born by means other than sex or Sex Magick. Any project or goal that you complete by means of loving and dedicated effort is a Magickal Child. This includes works of art, organizations, situations, etc.

Human myths hold stories of non-humans mating with humans. In the Bible, we are told that "The Nephilim were in the earth in those days, and also after that, when the sons of God came in unto the daughters of men, and they bore children to them; the same were the mighty men that were of old, the men of renown."(Gen. 6:4)

In Greco-Roman myth, Zeus/ Jupiter fathered heroes and demigods on human females; he used many disguises to do this, such as a swan, a bull, and even a shower of gold. In India, Krishna multiplied himself for the delight of the Gopi girls. There are European traditions of the King coupling with the Goddess for the welfare of the tribe, and even within Christianity, nuns are called "the brides of Christ."

While it's still possible to invoke a divine partner, Maat Magick holds that mating with extraterrestrials opens doorways leading to unthought-of, essentially NEW ways of seeing, knowing and understanding. Congress with gods can only reinforce present states of consciousness because gods are created in the image and likeness of Man. The human pantheons are self- referential and are closed systems, as it were.

For this type of Working, your Temple should be dark, but

incense and music, particularly New Age or "ambient" music are helpful. Begin by projecting a call on the Astral planes for entities interested in joining with you for mutual benefit and knowledge. Command your watches and wards to screen out undesirable types, such as Lower Astral ghosts and vampires, malicious or interfering beings. It's helpful to have a cup or chalice of water on the altar.

Stand and sway in the dark before the altar, making enticing, but wordless sounds with your voice. Envision yourself rising from the earth into space, out beyond our solar system, above the plane of our galaxy and moving toward its center. Become aware of every part of your skin, aware of the nerve endings in it; pay attention to your sense of touch and stimulate it until you are sensitive to the slightest movement of air.

When you feel the presence of the Other, open yourself to it and follow its instructions, insofar as they do not conflict with your Will. Beyond this, follow the rite to its conclusion. If the Other so indicates, drink the water as its charged Sacrament.

At this point, let's visit the Second Chakra, the Svadhisthana, in the same way that we visited the Muladhara in our last session. Relax, but keep your spine straight, close your eyes, and envision your point of consciousness behind your eyes. Move backward in your skull, down your cerebellum and brain stem, down your spinal cord to its end.

At the Muladhara Chakra, become aware of Kundalini, the fire snake coiled at the base of your spine. Focus on this bright serpent, and move with it up to the next Chakra, that of the genitals, the Svadhisthana. This nexus of energy spins slowly when you're calm and more quickly when you're aroused, a whirlpool of light that warms your sexual organs.

Open your Astral eyes to the world outside your body from this Chakra and look around the room. You probably will be aware of everyone else's Svadhisthana at this point, but don't be embarrassed; we are all vessels of the little god DNA, and this is just a demonstration of its power.

Trace the lines of influence from the genitals to other parts of your body, your mind, your past personal history and the decisions that you've made. Invoke Maat as honesty, then list the incidents in your life that were based on sexual desire and pursuit, but that you rationalized as logical or aesthetic choices. The point is to recognize the directing force of the instinct of sex, how all-pervasive it is, how we all are constructed to serve the goals of our genetic structure.

Focus your point of consciousness in the center of the Chakra-wheel and commune with the double helix of DNA. Open yourself to the understanding of the chemical bonds that shape this molecular assemblage, to the atoms and their particles that create and serve the necessity of life as we know it on our planet. Immerse yourself in the ocean of energy that coagulates into matter in accordance with subtle laws that gnaw on the edges of your comprehension. Feel the force of these laws without trying to analyze them; simply absorb the experience.

Follow the sequences through time of particles acquiring complexity through arranging themselves into atoms, of atoms uniting for greater complexity of molecules, of molecules shaping themselves into long chains, bending and bowing to the imperatives of electrical charges and attractions. Participate in the molecules growing, marrying and manipulating other substances, becoming viruses, bacteria, and cells. Experience the increasing sophistication of cells developing nuclei and cytoplasm, incorporating mitochondria, specializing into functional tissues, organs and structures.

Note how the DNA itself becomes more complex as its extensions multiply, how beneficial experiments are retained in its records while failures are erased by their own shortcomings. Behold the development of neurons and the appearance of ever more complex parts of the brain. Feel and watch the electric interplay of the neurons, the storms of thought, sensation and command that wash around and through all parts of the brain and nervous system.

Trace all the connections you can find between the brain and the genitals, then contemplate the rise and development of family, tribe, clan, nation, state and empire; consider the history of art, science and engineering throughout the ages, the rise and fall of religions, philosophies, trade routes and economic systems, then ask yourself: how much of all this exists to serve DNA and its desire to combine with itself in infinite variety? (The instructor should allow three minutes of silence at this point, and then continue.)

You now have some idea of the power of the Forgotten One of Sex, the directives of our DNA manifesting through our genitals. As Magickians, we should remember always this dynamo available for our Magick. We should also remember that all Magickal Children should be begotten under Will; casual, undirected sex pollutes the Astral planes and wastes precious resources. Your own meditations on the subject will convince you more firmly of these points than could any words from me.

Slowly, withdraw your point of consciousness from the Svadhisthana Chakra and move it up your spinal cord, through your brain stem and back to its usual position behind your eyes. Pay attention to your breathing, bring it to your regular rate and then slowly open your eyes.

I've kept our discussion focused on eighth degree, solitary Workings. It's only sensible to begin your work in this area alone, even if you have a regular sexual partner. You have to become familiar with the way the energies work, with the Willed direction of your Magick, before you try to teach another person about it. Autoeroticism is a limited method, compared with what can be accomplished with a competent partner, although the range of effectiveness of eighth degree work is impressively wide.

As an assignment, I'd like you to practice formulating your Will on a topic of your choice in a sigil, as I described earlier. To review: first, formulate your desire as a sentence. Strike through the second, third and so on repetitions of all letters. Take the remaining letters and form them into an abstract design that

doesn't look like a word. The resulting design is a sigil of your Will.

The sexual part of your practice I leave entirely up to you, since each person knows his or her own body best. Enjoy your experiments and exercises with this Chakra. Please be very careful about the intentions you focus upon in Working with it, since Magick does work and Sex Magick works extremely well.

LECTURE 4

Welcome to the fourth lecture on Kundalini and Maat Magick. In our previous meetings, we discussed the nature and the purposes of Magick in general and of Maat Magick in particular, Temple requirements for the physical part of Magick, Sex Magick and the nature of our two lower Chakras. We also investigated the nature of the Forgotten Ones of Hunger and Sex.

Today we will explore the Forgotten One of Fight or Flight, the third lowest Chakra, the Manipura, and the Martial applications of Magick.

The history of the human race is the history of invasions, wars, conquests and domination. Peace seems to be a time of relative calm between conflicts, an interruption of the norm. Why is this so? No other species, with the exception of certain ants, bees and wasps, practice mass combat. What is there in our nature that promotes, and even ensures, that certain groups of us do battle with each other?

Other animal species share our Forgotten One, our instinct for fighting a threat or fleeing from danger, but only humanity has developed it to the mass phenomenon of war.

The strength and size of our fight/flight instinct, I believe, results from its combination with other survival urges: those of Hunger, Clanning, and to smaller degree, Sex. It also seems that the little god DNA encourages war among us in order to control our numbers and protect the diversity of other orders of life on

our planet.

The development of human intelligence enabled us to kill off our major predators, construct shelter from the elements, and increase our numbers and lifespans. Whether through the gathering of wild plants, hunting, herding, or agriculture, each individual needs a certain amount of land to provide food for him or her.

When there were so many of us in a given region that the food supply began to fail, we moved on to new territories. This strategy is good until we began finding other people already established in the territories.

Our increasing intelligence sometimes produced cooperation instead of conflict, as in the invention of irrigation systems, in order to make more efficient use of resources and ease the pressure to migrate. More often, our primitive intelligence argued that it's easier to take the products of other people's work than to do the work ourselves. This thinking led to slavery as well as to war, and today it takes the form of multinational corporations using the cheapest labor available in developing countries.

Warfare seems to have evolved through the millennia from simple rapine and pillage, through control of territory, which includes eliminating rivals for leadership, as in wars, and foreign conquests, to war in support of allies of the proper ideological leanings. There have been wars over religions, like the Christian Crusades and Islamic Jihads, as well as one-sided campaigns against heretics, witches and Jews. In the Twentieth Century, with the development and use of the atomic bomb, war had reached the level of possibly annihilating the human race.

Forty years ago, plus or minus, I was experiencing the first of the visions, or channelings, that developed into Maat Magick. At that time, the USA and the Soviet Union were poised on the brink of nuclear war; my sources called the situation a crisis node, one of those crossroads where the choices made would create the nature of its future. My contact-entity, N'Aton, gave me methods and concepts which, used in Magick, would get

us through the crisis and begin the manifestation of the new species, Homo veritas.

Our numbers, knowledge and technology demand a change in our understanding of the Forgotten One of fight or flight; its traditional employment has become too dangerous both for the human race and for planet Earth.

Homo veritas won't continue all of the practices of Homo sapiens; individual and collective violence is the first thing to be rid of.

Maat Magick is a Magick of transition, and its practitioners have the duty of shaping the course that global events will follow. Even though the greatest danger of nuclear destruction has been abated, there remain numerous wars and individual violences throughout the world.

In order to grasp the problem, we must come to an accurate understanding of the Mars-force, of the urgings of the Manipura Chakra, and of the belligerent nature of humanity.

The fight-or-flight instinct should be called, perhaps, by another name that doesn't limit action to two choices. Its survival value lies in removing the individual from danger, but it has expanded to include removing other people from danger, and to initiating attacks, be it in robbery, assassination, or warfare. When its action manifests in groups, it combines cooperation with competition.

We often see such combinations in non-human Nature. Forests and jungles have plants competing for sunlight and soil nutrients, but trees send each other chemical warnings about insect infestations. Ant colonies often wage warfare against each other, but some ants herd and milk aphids like humans milk cows.

Individually, we are inefficient predators, with small teeth and flat nails instead of claws, naked skin and a relatively slow running speed. In groups, and using killing tools, we hunted mastodon, mammoth and bison, and defended ourselves and our families against tigers and wolves.

In our human beginnings, we needed individual and collective killing and wounding techniques in order to survive. As our numbers increased, the way the Manipura energies manifested grew more complex, and came to serve purposes that overcame any sense of species kinship. Let's see if we can organize these ways and purposes as they exist today.

This list of forms of human aggression may help us to see the varieties of Martial force we're capable of using.

• One against one: assault, assassination/murder, duel, personal combat (I see personal combat as less formal than a duel.)

• One against few: terrorism, sabotage, hostage-taking, counting coup.

• One against many: terrorism, sabotage, hostage-taking

• Few against one: assault, manhunt, torture

• Few against few: melee, ambush, raid, skirmish

• Few against many: guerrilla warfare, revolution

• Many against one: lynching, execution

• Many against few: pogrom, genocide

• Many against many: war

You may be able to think of more instances of violence that humanity indulges in. Please add to this list whatever else you can think of.

I venture to guess that most people, when asked, would deplore all of these human activities, and would strive to

eliminate them whenever possible, yet history continues to be written in terms of conflict and conquest. We try to avoid violence for ourselves and for those we know and love, but somehow we agree that violence is permitted against the Enemy, the evil Other, in order to protect our own.

In most societies, the Warrior is the Hero; the War Leader often becomes the King, and his generals become Lords of the conquered lands as a reward for their support of the Leader. As tribal and clan warfare became more complex, the military profession was born. Peaceful farmers, tradespeople, artisans and priests were willing to support specialists in violence, to admire them, and to elevate them to civil leadership, in some cases. In other societies, the Warriors served a civilian King, a priestly class, or parliament.

Some science fiction writers surmise that we might need our capacity to fight in the event that invaders from space arrive to conquer us. Others speculate that we were engineered by a master species from space to be guardians of the planet we live on, and that our aggression was deliberately designed, much as we breed certain types of large dogs as guardians. I think that it's simpler and closer to the truth to say that DNA was convinced of aggression's usefulness to human survival by the fact that aggressors survive to breed.

Let's venture to our Manipura Chakras to see what we can find out about that center in ourselves. Please sit comfortably and close your eyes. Begin with sounding OM three times. The pronunciation is "Aaauuummnnng", holding the sound as long as possible.

Loosen your point of consciousness from its usual seat behind your eyes; see your surroundings by the light of your own radiance as a point. Move to the back of your skull, through your cerebellum and down your brainstem to your spinal cord. Slide gently all the way down to your first Chakra, the Muladhara, and watch it slowly spin as a four-petaled lotus of light.

Rise to your second Chakra, the Svadhisthana, bathing in

the flame of the fire serpent, Kundalini. Feel the force of the energy as it turns the six-petaled lotus to spin; feel the force of the spinning add itself to the current of flame.

Rise with Kundalini to the third Chakra, the Manipura, a rotating lotus of light with ten petals. Look beyond your body from this position, see what you can of the room and its furnishings. Call your attention back to the Chakra itself, and move yourself to its center, feeling its forces spin about you.

These forces are very strong. Your Manipura can move in a limited span; its range is from the solar plexus, near your diaphragm, to a spot about 4 to 5cm. below your navel. Your Chi force lives here, the force you learn to concentrate and use in the practice of the Oriental Martial Arts. Endurance and determination live here too.

Without straining your astral sight, look for lines of force emanating from the Manipura, radiating upward to your head and arms and downward to your feet. The lines to and from your lungs and heart should show more clearly than the others; these lines feed prana, or life force, from your breathing to your Manipura, which translates the prana into the energy that animates your physical body and its echoes on other planes.

Note how your entire Manipura Chakra pulses in time to your breathing. Follow the prana-flow from the Manipura to the adrenal glands atop your kidneys, then back again. Feel how the energy of the universe circulates within you, filling your body with strength and vigor. Slow your breathing, and note how the lotus of the Chakra spins more slowly. Speed up your breathing and see how the lotus spins more quickly. You can arouse or calm the Manipura by means of the speed and quality of your breathing. This is another thing that needs to be practiced in order to understand and use it properly.

Slowly withdraw your consciousness back into your spinal cord and rise again to your skull and your familiar home behind your eyes. Extend your awareness through your body, then open your eyes.

With some practice, and concentration, you can project streamers of force from the Manipura out into the material world to help you in a physical task. If you ever go hiking in hill country, you can practice using your Chi force to help your body climb. As you begin a climb, focus your attention on your Manipura and visualize lines of light flowing from your abdomen. Wrap them around a tree or a boulder above you and pull yourself up the lines as you climb. It should make lighter work for your arms and legs. Carlos Castaneda depicts a Yaqui shaman using this technique to climb a waterfall.

Try using the Chi/Manipura for other situations; if you have to lift a heavy object, project the energy under the object and extend it upwards; if you need to push a wheeled vehicle, extend the energy and push with it as well as with your hands.

Another interesting exercise is to ask a friend to try to push you off the place on which you are standing. This isn't a difficult thing to do, since our two-footed stance isn't very stable. Then, focus on your Manipura and send lines of force down through your feet and into the earth (even if they have to pass through a building or pavement), making them branch like the roots of a tree. Join your energy with that of the earth, then ask your friend to try to push you again.

The point of these exercises is to become familiar with the Manipura and with the force of its Forgotten One. It's also a good thing to become acquainted with its darker aspects.

First, banish and seal your Temple. Imagine an enemy, from any time in your life, under any circumstances. This person should be one who has done you some harm, or has harmed someone you love, or has done other serious wrong that has hurt you.

Now think of that person as being only half a meter tall, and helpless in your presence. Feel the force of your wrath directed toward him or her, and visualize yourself tearing him or her to pieces. Pay close attention to how you feel. Is there a sensation of satisfaction and pleasure in the violence?

What you experience in this exercise is the dark emotion of vengeance. The Nightside of Maat is Lex Talionis, the "eye for an eye and a tooth for a tooth" of our barbarian past. If you have difficulty in raising wrath on your enemy because of your natural character or training, invoke the Berserker spirit, or battle-madness of the ancient Norse, the Celts, or any of the early conquerors. When this experiment is complete, banish your Temple and unseal its boundaries.

As a species, we have invented a few ways to use the Manipura energies in non-violent ways. We have sports, on the individual and on the team level. We also have literature, art, theater, cinema and other media which provide vicarious ways that people can experience the satisfactions of violence without harming themselves or others. Hard physical labor and exercise are other ways to employ the Manipura energy, although machines have replaced humans in many fields of physical work.

The stress and tension of modern life, from our crowding together in cities and trying to make a living, to a sense of being powerless before tyrannical people like some parents, teachers, and bosses, press on our Manipura. Unable to strike directly at the sources of our aggravation, we sometimes resort to domestic violence of spouse and child battering, harming animals, or picking fights in bars. Many times we strike at people who are of a different race, national background or religion since they seem to be apt targets for our frustrated wrath.

As Magickians, we have the opportunity to direct the Manipura energy of ourselves and of others to the service of species evolution. We do this by means of Temple rites, by example in daily life, and by acting as living talismans for the rest of humanity.

In the course of formulating Maat Magick, I constructed a Tree of Life in which the Sephiroth were assigned titles of Maat as a godform. In Geburah (Strength), the Sphere of Mars, she is named Air, the Unconfined. This seems an odd assignment, since air is not usually associated with strength. In fact, to call

something "airy" means that it lacks substance or weight, isn't serious, and can have little effect on anything.

If you think about it, though, air's strength is obvious. Its properties allow birds, bats, and aircraft to fly; as atmosphere, it supports the metabolism of the vast majority of life on earth, with the exception of anaerobic bacteria. Its mixture of gasses serves both vegetable and animal life. The atmosphere is where weather and climate occur; who could argue against the power of the hurricane, tornado, gale or thunderstorm?

Air is present everywhere on our planet, at various densities, and at the same time is invisible and impalpable, except for when it moves. Air is also a form of prana that we inhale, a force that we share with the universe. Air is the medium by which we speak, by which we convey our words and our Word of Magickal command.

In Chaos Science, the 'butterfly effect' is a metaphor for the delicacy of initial conditions of turbulence. It says that a butterfly flapping its wings in China could begin a minor air current that builds into a storm that ravages the west coast of North America and beyond. In like manner, your Word of Will, spoken in ritual in a focused way, can roll around the world to inspire change in the hearts of the whole human race. Although a Magickal Word fades from physical hearing at a certain distance and with the lapse of time, the Astral body of the atmosphere carries it onward in an undiminished wave.

At this point in our instructional series, it would be best to work on ourselves as individuals in coming to terms with our own Martial forces, and then, where possible, with other people. As individuals, we can construct a well-sealed Temple ritual in which to evoke the Forgotten One of Fight or Flight as an entity and wrestle with it much as Jacob wrestled with an angel in the Bible tale.

Contending with an Other in the wrestling style gives you a chance to know him, her, or it in a way that's almost as intimate as sex. You can follow the moves of your Astral and etheric bodies

with identical moves in your physical body, so that you seem to dance.

I leave the details of your ritual construction up to you. A very useful book for ritual construction is Aleister Crowley's Liber 777. The tables in it can provide traditional choices of colors, incenses, timing, etc. Otherwise, your own artistic senses can guide you to the best means to focus your attention on your rite in Temple. I do suggest that you include the following in a Maatian Martial rite:

• A thorough banishing and sealing of the Temple

• A color scheme of red and black

• The presence of iron in the Temple

• A feather (from a rooster, if possible) as a symbol of Maat.

If you can find an instructor in the Oriental Martial Arts, such as Tai Chi Chuan, Akido, Tae Kwan Do, Kung Fu, etc., it would be good to become his or her student. In addition, an interesting exercise for two people is 'Sticky Hands'.

To do this, face your partner; slowly and gently, try to touch his or her body while blocking him or her from touching yours, while he or she does the same to you. Keep your hands in contact with those of your partner, moving them constantly in circles and curves. When you think your partner isn't paying attention, try to move a hand away from his or hers to land a body touch.

As the attunement between the two of you grows, you will come to feel and anticipate each other's moves, and will develop perfect blocking. Avoid the tendency to speed up and increase force in your movements, so that touches do not become blows and so that anger is not aroused. The two main benefits of such an exercise are the awareness of Chi in yourself and in your

partner, and the calm control of it.

As we become better acquainted with the higher Chakras and the more developed Forgotten Ones, we will become better able to put the Manipura in balance and under control. This center of power has protected our species from before its beginnings, and can still serve us well if we adapt it to current conditions.

LECTURE 5

I n the first four lectures, we covered material about Maat Magick, Magick in general, the three lower Chakras, and the Forgotten Ones, or survival instincts and urges that operate with and through them.

There are humans living now who operate primarily through their three lower Chakras, leaving their upper Chakras inactivated. The upper Chakras automatically function at a minimum level to keep such people alive and sometimes self-supporting, but generally these people do not interact with others well, and do not understand the essence of the Golden Rule: "Do unto others as you would have them do unto you."

For them, the Golden Rule is, "Whoever has the gold makes the rules."

According to some schools of esoteric thought, entities from simpler and more primitive levels of existence incarnate into the human species as a natural step in universal spiritual evolution. Until such entities learn the rules and customs of being human, they operate only on the principles of self-preservation and the pursuit of pleasure. They are often attractive and clever, but these "First-time Elementals" behave in ways that demonstrate a lack of ethics and sympathy.

For many more people, the fourth Chakra, the Anahata, is activated to a greater or lesser degree by experience with the action of other Chakras; maternal love, sexual attraction turned romantic, family loyalty, etc. The Forgotten One of the Heart

Chakra is the Clanning instinct, the method of mutual survival suited to an individually defenseless mammal.

The little god inside us, DNA, seems to operate on two primary principles: continuity and variety. We are designed to preserve our own lives, to desire to mate, to defend our families and ourselves and to provide for their sustenance and welfare. Given the fact that humans take a relatively longer time to reach maturity than any other species on earth, we need an urge or instinct that operates on a long-term basis to provide the extended care our offspring require.

I call this urge the Clanning instinct; it's the Forgotten One that operates from the Anahata Chakra, and it serves to bind together parents, siblings, grandparents, uncles, aunts and cousins into units of mutual help and support. Humans are at a physiological disadvantage compared to many of the animals we share the planet with—we have no hooves, horns, claws or fangs—and so we depend on other things for our survival. These things include rational thought, language, planning and cooperative action.

The Clanning instinct directs us to give high priority to the survival of those who share our particular configurations of DNA: close relatives, and those accepted into our families through marriage. This instinct appears in animals other than humans, to a greater or lesser degree. With ants, termites, bees and the naked mole rats of Africa, only one female produces young, but the other members of the colony work together at food-gathering, housekeeping and defense of the whole. Elephants, apes and chimpanzees live together, their numbers providing protection for the group. Among wolves and certain wild dogs, only the Alpha couples reproduce, but all members hunt to provide for the cubs. The human race, with its relatively feeble physical endowments, relies heavily on the Forgotten One of Clanning.

In the human case, DNA has added a bias toward exogamy, a strong inclination to mate with someone outside the immediate

family. While inbreeding has been used occasionally to protect the purity of certain royal lines, as in Pharaonic Egypt and in old Hawaii, we have generally avoided the problem of unfavorable double recessive traits. To make it possible to find a mate outside the immediate family, the Clanning instinct extends itself to counter our tendency to xenophobia.

In the course of human history, the protection of Clanning has extended itself to enable the formation of tribes, states and nations. Other influences, such as the Forgotten One of fight or flight, have limited this extension, so that we still have wars, revolutions, social classes and race prejudice. One of the aims and effects of Maat Magick is to extend the range of the Heart Chakra to include all of humanity and the other species of life with which we share this planet as a first stage.

There are those who think that an integrated planet, with all its systems running harmoniously, would be a bore without conflict to fuel interest and Art. I would agree with that view were it not for the fact that the beginnings of the double consciousness marking our next evolutionary stage are but preparations for our meeting, knowing and working with non-terrestrial beings. If an integrated humanity, functioning as the nerve system of Earth, were to remain planet-bound forever, we would indeed perish from boredom. However, we have work waiting for us that requires us to redirect and control our Third Chakra xenophobia. First we practice and succeed among ourselves, and then we'll be in shape for those who wait.

The Anahata Chakra, the nexus of the heart, is a gateway that shares aspects of our prehuman ancestors and the realizations of our developing intelligence as humans. The benefits of mutual cooperation lie with our ancestors, and the phenomenon of love lies with our evolving intelligence. Love has been defined many times by religion, art and psychology. It's been called the desire for unity, the wishing of good to the beloved, the placing of a higher value upon the beloved than on oneself.

Love as we know it depends on the duality of self and Other,

and on the yearning to replace that duality with unity and/or nothingness. In our dualistic view of life, the unity that love gives us is a joining of two (or more) separate beings into a higher order of existence, an acting in concert, a sharing of joy, pleasure, and satisfying work. From the spiritual viewpoint, love is the removal of the illusion of separation, a dissolving of the barriers between and among the manifestations of Divine Intelligence.

Love is a reaching beyond the self of Ego, an inclusion of another in our regard for ourselves. There are many faces of love, ranging in a spectrum from biological reaction (falling in love) to the spiritual response to a higher good (self-sacrifice). There are also other emotions that claim to be love, but are not.

Gratitude and pleasure are the bases of children's love of parents; it's a natural response to those who pay attention to us, satisfy our hunger, keep our bodies comfortable and share their warmth, heartbeat and aura. The sharing of place, time and parental regard is the base of siblings' love for each other.

There's also an admixture of competition and jealousy from the Manipura Chakra, but in healthy families where parents exhibit no favoritism, love can win in most situations.

The love of friendship is intimate without being sexual, in most cases. It can begin in early childhood and continue to the grave.

A friend is one who understands you, shares secrets with you, and helps you in many ways. There are those who say that the love of friendship is a higher type of love than a love that includes, or is based upon, sexual intimacy. Some of the difficulties of other types of love, such as jealousy and taking advantage of the other person's feelings of kindness, can happen in friendships.

Resolving such difficulties strengthens love, even though both difficulties and their resolutions change the love to some degree.

With the onset of puberty, we become vulnerable to romantic love, to the schoolchild crush, the confusion of desire and

desirability, the pain and angst of coming to grips with a whole new way of living that childhood only faintly foreshadowed. Even though the other types of love that we've just mentioned have definite power for change, the love combined with desire provides a dynamo of Magickal energy, provided that Will directs the love.

Maat Magick is a Thelemic Magick, that is, the formula of Love under Will is the foundation and primary premise of Maat Magick. I suggest that you read the works of Aleister Crowley for a full exposition of Love under Will, but the essence of the formula can be stated in the aphorism: Love without Will is sentimentality; Will without Love is tyranny. Although distinct entities in one state of consciousness, Love and Will equal each other in another state of consciousness.

In the worlds of dualism, the Magickian must put all types of love under the direction of will, or the Magick will be weakened and diverted from its purpose. This includes the types of love already mentioned, plus love of committed partners, love of family in general, patriotism, love of the universe and love of abstract concepts like honor, truth and God, however God is seen.

As you develop your abilities to use the various methods of Magick and Mysticism, take the time to make an inventory list of all your loves, from people and places to things and ideas. How many kinds of love have you experienced? How many kinds of love do you know about? Make another list of your hates. In combination, the lists will give you a good idea of the web of connection and attachments in which you live. The idea is for you to be the spider in the web, not the fly. Hate is the negative aspect of love, not its opposite. The opposite of love is indifference.

In order to put Love under Will, the Magickian has to know what his or her individual Will is. I have found that neophytes in Magick spend a lot of time and frustration trying to find out what their Will is. The situation reflects that of the student who

has to choose a specialized course of education to fit him or her for a career or profession. What is it that you want to do with your life? It would be wonderful if we could all be professional Magickians, but since the essence of Magick belongs to each individual, and since you can't really change someone else, there's no mundane market for the High Art.

There are those who make money casting horoscopes or doing Tarot readings or removing curses, etc., but these practices are just putting the tools of Magick at the disposal of uninitiates for a price. The choices we make about careers or jobs in the Outer should employ our talents and proficiencies and take care of our necessary living expenses. The choices we make about personal relationships should take care of our emotional and biological needs, and the type of introspective processes we choose to practice should take care of our spiritual needs. All these choices are parts of Will, and our Magick should permeate all fields of activity.

As a general principle, our Will directs us to action and thoughts that assist our growth and development in all fields of life. As we gain broader perspectives and a more comprehensive context for our role in life, our definition of Will changes. Situations arise that force a choice; we consult our Will to see how the options would assist or hinder it.

A true idea of one's Will is the fruit of self-knowledge. There comes a point in our course of self-knowledge where our Will expands its concerns beyond our personal welfare and embraces other humans, our planet, and the Universe at large. Our Magick shifts its emphasis from the gathering of information to the formulation of solutions for the problems of our species and our planet.

Science has changed our views, over the centuries, from seeing humanity as the "crown of Creation" and the Earth as the center of the Cosmos to realizing we're one species among many in a complex web of food chains, symbiosis and parasitism living on a planet orbiting a modest yellow star in the outer reaches of

one galaxy among many. Maat Magick encourages us to begin to function more as a responsible species in the context of the Earth at large, to become the neural net of the planet, to restore the environment to a new balance and health.

On the individual level, though, we are each the center of the Universe, each the heart of the world to ourselves. It is through the expansion of our centrality that we arrive at the state of true Will and true Love. This does not mean an expansion of the Ego that considers everyone and everything "outside" of us our possession or property, existing for our personal enhancement.

Rather, the idea of who we are extends itself beyond our skin to infinity, making the Biblical injunction "Love thy neighbor as thyself" a constant part of life. It's important to establish the broadest possible view of ourselves in order to keep our Magick true and effective.

Let's visit our Anahata Chakra to see what we can learn of it, and what we can learn of our Will and our Love.

Sit comfortably and close your eyes. Become aware of your location behind your eyes; become aware of the structures around you in the glowing light of your awareness. Move toward the back of your skull, back and down, through your cerebellum and brain stem, down your spinal cord to the end of your spine. Here are familiar places; the Muladhara, wherein is based Kundalini, the Firesnake of energy that animates your physical body. The lotus of the Chakra spins with light, playing with energy to and from Kundalini. The serpent begins to rise.

As it rises, Kundalini touches your second Chakra, the Svadhisthana, and sets its lotus wheel spinning faster. You become aware of the power of your genitals and aware of their Magickal nature. The Svadhisthana returns energy to the Firesnake, more energy than it received, and Kundalini rises higher. Near your navel now, it touches your third Chakra, the Manipura, and your readiness for action increases as the Chakra lotus increases the speed of its spin. The rotation of this energy-wheel acts as a gyroscope to balance your strength and power, and feeds more

energy into the Kundalini, which rises to the heart Chakra, the Anahata.

This lotus of light pulses as it spins, keeping time with the beating of your physical heart. Move to the center of the lotus, the middle of the Anahata. The center is a still point, a mote of eternity amid the rhythm that counts the passage of time. This still point is the meeting ground between you and your secret Self, your Genius, your Daemon that Crowley calls your Holy Guardian Angel. From this point emanates Love, the essence of coherence and connection that makes you and the Cosmos a single thing of life and joy. The emanating itself, as well as the outward flow of Love, is Will.

Position your point of awareness exactly on the mote of eternity, and then flow with the tides of Love. You expand with the expansion of Love, riding with it as it embraces your physical body, the chair you sit in, the air, the furniture and the people in the room.

Love flows through the floor and down the walls of the building, into the earth, spreading until it fills the planet. Love flows out and up into the air, rejoicing in the birds, the insects, the clouds, the winds. It flows from Earth to join with the moon, the other planets and asteroids, the sun, and all the stars and wonders that swim in outer space.

You lose your name in the Will-flow of Love; you melt into bliss, touching and blending with all things that are, or could possibly come to be. Only your physical body anchors you here, radiating its signals of need that precipitate your awareness out from the trance of Cosmic Love. You remember where you are: in the center of your Anahata Chakra in the center of your heart in the center of your body. You return to yourself with a glow and warmth that pulses in time with your heart and its Chakra.

Slowly you move back into your spinal cord. You rest like a jewel in the crown of Kundalini, which now rises by itself, bringing you back to your home in your brain. Slowly you settle into the place behind your eyes, open your eyes, and stretch

your body gently.

This Anahata meditation is a good preliminary practice for any Magickal ritual you undertake to perform. It reminds you of your connection with all things, your constant Magickal Link with the Cosmos and with all things in it. Although it's good to have a physical Link in Magick worked for manifestation, the universal connection we have with all things will help us in our causing change in those things.

One difficulty that may arise with the realization of universal Love is a feeling of frustration and helplessness at the magnitude and quantity of changes needed to help our species and the planet at large. There are so many people doing stupid things that harm themselves and everyone else that the problem of "what's wrong with the world" seems too much for any individual to help. In addition to human meddling, Nature itself holds many deadly events that can kill us, injure us, and destroy what we've built. What's a Magickian to do?

The first act is to remember the connections of Love and Will that you experience in the heart Chakra meditations. The connections ensure that your intentions, actions and decisions will affect the rest of the world. They make you a living talisman whose development influences the development of all other people and things. This talismanic connection is an awesome responsibility, but if you are Maat, if you are in balance and truth with yourself and the Cosmos, your life will be beneficial and your Work will be reflected in world change.

The second act is to become familiar with Chaos Theory, in which you will learn that the turbulent waves of change on every plane depend on initial conditions, small and insignificant though they seem. The right act at the right time, whether it be formal ritual, the creation of art of any kind, informal conversation, a letter to the editors of a newspaper, and so on, can begin a cascade of events that profoundly change the world. The more information, understanding and wisdom that you bring to your Work, the better its chances are to succeed.

The third act is to join with your colleagues in concerted action, both Inner and Outer, to begin a change and take it as far as you can. The possibilities are endless. By colleagues, I don't mean only the other members of the class and your Instructor, but also those people who will be drawn to you by your charisma and radiance from your Heart Chakra.

I have seen this phenomenon operate in different places at different times: as soon as a person begins to follow his or her interest in the field of the Occult, people who are hungry for esoteric knowledge begin to show up. These people can be friends of friends, strangers encountered in bookshops and cafes, or old acquaintances who develop such interests suddenly. The neophyte Occultist often feels uncomfortable with sharing information but newly acquired. How can you teach what you barely know?

We muddle through with what we know, and do our best, since we do not own what we learn. When you begin operating from the Heart Chakra, the people drawn to your orbit usually screen themselves into two main categories: those whose interest isn't strong enough to promote the hard work involved in Magick, and those who know they have found their true calling. Even among the sincere, there often arises problems with Ego; if the people involved in disputes can rise above any quarreling and contention, the problems dissolve in the course of the work.

A thing to remember about the heart and its Chakra and its Forgotten One of Clanning is this: you will have no need to seek out other people to teach, for they will find you. Magickians do not preach on street corners nor try to recruit other people into the practice of Magick. The esoteric knowledge of Magick and Mysticism should not be sold, promoted, or even made too easy to find.

Your responsibility to the Great Work requires that you work on your own development, refinement and abilities. Your job is to prepare yourself for whatever circumstances the Cosmos brings your way. You have to recognize what is your business and

what is not, what things need your intervention and what things will work themselves out without you. The natural impulse of a generous heart is to share immediately a good new thing with the people it cares about, and to save as many people as possible from pain and suffering. Because there are layers and levels of truth, however, you must learn discernment in order to find where the greater good lies in any situation.

I have an assignment for each of you, an exercise in practice of what we have discussed today. I want you to find someone who needs help and give it to him or her. The type of help needed and given can be in any form—money, time, information or physical work. You can know the person you select or he or she can be a stranger. In giving your help, make it clear that the person is doing you the favor of allowing you to help. If the person tries to pay you or to return the favor, ask that he or she help someone else and make the same request to pass it on.

Your help can be something small, like assisting someone to carry packages, or it can be something more substantial like reading to a blind person or caring for someone's child or sick relative for a few hours so the caregiver can have a break. If you can't find anyone to help, contact a social-service agency, or a church.

Your help can be a one-time thing, or you can make a commitment for continuing your help over time. Whatever you choose, write it in your Magickal Record, and track your actions, feelings and observations for two weeks. During these two weeks, visit your Anahata Chakra at least once a day. At the end of that time, please write a summary of your experience in your Magickal Record.

LECTURE 6

Welcome to our sixth lecture in our series on Maat Magick. Today we'll discuss our instinct to speak and listen to each other, the Forgotten One of Communication. This urge is centered in the throat, in the Vishuda Chakra. In Maat Magick, as in other forms of Magick, the power of the Word is paramount in launching the force of Will into action for change. Humanity is not the only species to communicate among itself. Elephants trumpet and rumble, whales and porpoises whistle and click, crickets chirp, and even trees and other plants communicate chemically. Humans can form words and develop languages because our mouth, throat and lungs are constructed in such a way as to permit a huge variety of sounds to be produced. Our brains are complex enough to use the versatile instrument of our voice to express abstract thought, mathematical concepts and the nuances of feelings.

The instruments of speech also permit us to sing and to chant, to combine words and music into an Art that can move and inspire both the singer and the listener. We are also able to translate the spoken word into the written word by a marvelous mental process that establishes, for an indefinite time, information that would disappear with the disappearance of memory and the listeners who heard it.

Current technology permits us to record and play back song and speech as well as images of the singer or speaker. We have

the cell phone, radio, television and the Internet to take our words almost anywhere in the world. The printing press and its modern successors allow us to distribute many copies of our written words, and the postal services of different countries permit us to correspond with people around the world.

In Magick, the use of the word, spoken aloud in ritual, begins a set of vibrations in the Astral and Etheric worlds that affect the seeds of manifestation, no matter the distance and no matter the time. This isn't just a matter of the psychological condition the Magickian enters in ritual circumstances; rather, the effectiveness of words—and of Words of Power—relies on the ma kheru, or the True Voice of the Magickian.

The ma kheru is one of the most important tools and talents of the Magickian. The term itself is Egyptian, and it has several layers of meaning. As the True Voice, it is the sound with which we express our True Will; since nothing can interfere, ultimately, with the manifestation of True Will, the voice itself achieves the irresistible power of that which it expresses. The ma kheru is also a production of a certain pitch and timbre that arises from the True Self, that is, the Self that has no identity, or Tao that moves through and with the True Voice. In the True Self, there is no Ego that could interfere with the flow of the Magickal Current.

In Maat Magick, the True Voice is that which speaks Maat, or Truth itself. There is a saying in Yoga that if you speak nothing but the truth for twelve years, then anything you speak will come true, will be true. The Maat Magickian must take this saying seriously if he or she intends to develop the ma kheru. Without its development, there is no Maat Magick.

Let us consider, for a moment, why our instinct for communication can be called a Forgotten One in a world that is filled with talk, announcements, conversations, arguments, political speeches, sermons and gossip. If we look at speech from the point of view of our little god DNA, we see in it a means of coordinating group effort on the hunt, of constructing fortifications around a village, of understanding the reports of

scouts on the nature and number of approaching enemies, of passing along to the children the knowledge and wisdom of the past.

Human life is too complex for each individual to learn everything he or she needs for survival on a trial and error basis. Speech enables us to share the benefits of our ancestors' mistakes and successes on a level that goes far beyond example, gesture and demonstration—although these are important adjuncts to speech.

Speech also teaches us those things which define our family, tribe and clan as Us: beliefs, rituals, taboos and obligations to the spirits and the ancestors. These things bind us together through our feelings as they lubricate social interactions among individuals. One of the cruelest punishments is "shunning", the refusal of the group to communicate with the individual being punished.

Speech became a Forgotten One with the telling of the first lie. By lie I mean a deliberate statement of something that is not so for the purpose of doing harm, avoiding blame or to get an advantage for personal gain. Myth, poetry, fiction, invisible childhood friends and personal visions are not lies; rather, they are specialized truths. Humans aren't the only species to practice deception. There are insects that masquerade as leaves, mother birds who pretend to have a broken wing in order to lead a predator away from the nest, and harmless snakes that closely resemble poisonous varieties. In some circumstances, human deceptions can be as innocent and as beneficial as those of animals, whether in life or death situations or just in being kind to the emotionally vulnerable.

Most lies aren't of the justified kind, however. Most human untruths are spoken to gratify the Ego, to enhance one's reputation, to undermine the good name of a rival, or to see just how gullible the listeners are. Even though all truths capable of being spoken are partial truths, relative truths, the vibrations of deliberate lies infect the non-physical planes with confusion and

obscurity. The Maat Magickian should realize, at the beginning of his or her Work, that speaking deliberate falsehoods undermines the effectiveness of the Magick, and can even produce results that are opposed to or harmful to the Magick's intent.

What do you do in a situation where speaking the truth could cause harm to oneself or another? The best option is silence, of course. Where silence could be as harmful as speech, though, there are some options that could apply. The "mental reservation" method lets you speak part of a truth aloud and finish it mentally. For example, if a person is looking for your friend with the intention of harming him or her, and this person asks you where your friend is, you might tell him "I really couldn't say" (and continue silently, "because if I did, I would be betraying a friendship".) Or you could say, "I have no idea" ("of the extent of the damage you would cause him.")

In situations where you are concerned about the results of speaking truth, remember that there are levels and degrees of truth, and it is permitted to evade telling a lesser truth in order to preserve a greater truth, but only in the light of careful ethical consideration. This applies even to minor situations where the truth would hurt the feelings of a person who is asking your opinion. If a proud grandmother shows you the photo of a truly ugly baby, you could say, "What a wonderful child!" because all living things are wonderful.

Situations that seem to require the manipulation of truth for a higher end are rare, and what you do about these situations depends on your understanding of the nature of truth.

I share the Egyptians' regard for Maat, the personified principle of truth, because she provides both a firm foundation for living and an ever-advancing goal that leads us, like the Holy Grail, on a great quest for knowledge, understanding and wisdom.

Truth is not only that which is so; it is the accurate reporting of that which is so, to the best of our understanding. Even though, in a metaphysical sense, we contain the Cosmos within

us, the body of human knowledge does not. Will we, as a genus, ever comprehend everything there is to know? At the present time, that seems unlikely. Even though our individual and collective grasp of the truth is partial and, in varying degrees, inaccurate, we have enough of it that our machines work, our mathematics can be proven by experiment, and civilization survives the passage of generations of us.

We also have the Body of Initiated Tradition, the occult truths of Magick and Mysticism compiled by generations of Initiates from their experiences in the field. Some of the truths are physiological (if you slow your breathing, your spirit becomes calm and your mind becomes clear). Others are psychological (if you concentrate your senses and your attention on an intended change in the Outer, you will change your Inner state in a parallel manner). Other truths are metaphysical (if you pursue the origin of anything, if you pursue the inmost essence of anything, if you pursue the vision of your True Self, you ultimately find that Nothing of which nothing true can be said).

The essence of truth is silence; only the unutterable is true. Yet we have a Voice, a Word, a Will within the complexity of existence, and even if all existence is illusion, we are ethically obliged to operate from the most complete state of truth of which we are capable. Magick itself deals with changing illusion, and so truth fragments when it appears in manifestation.

Much of Maat Magick consists of gathering up the shards of truth found in manifestation and fitting them together so they most closely resemble their original, unshattered state.

The shards of truth we find are holograms; each contains all the information of the original whole, but in a fuzzy, obscure fashion. The more fragments we find and combine with those we have, the more clearly we can envision the Truth of which they are parts. The information in each shard, if we can read it, gives us the directions on how to assemble them.

The rationality and intuition used in the assembly of Truth are functions of the Chakras above the Vishuda, but the

speaking of them remains centered in the throat. The initiate is responsible for speaking the truths of Initiation to the sincere enquirer; the manner of speaking should be the way that most clearly conveys the right meaning to the listener. Initiatory speech implies initiated listening. The time and circumstances in which you speak Initiatory truths to the enquirer are as important in conveying meaning as using language that he or she understands.

You learn right timing by honing your sensitivities to other people's state of mind, capacities, and the influences working upon them. To do this, clear your mind of your own thoughts, opinions and feelings, and concentrate fully upon the speaker.

While your physical ears hear the words and the tone of voice, you also observe posture, body language, and facial expressions. Your Astral ears hear the words behind the words, the hidden tensions and directions of which the speaker probably knows nothing.

Finally, on the level of the Anahata Chakra and of the Holy Guardian Angel, listen to what your Angel tells you about the speaker. In the vision of Duality, your Angel converses with the Angel of the speaker, and advice is relayed to you about the right time and manner to speak initiatory words to the speaker. In the vision that encompasses Duality but is not subject to it, the speaker's Angel and your Angel are the same. Right listening is a near-total attunement with the speaker's individual essence. When you are that attuned to someone, not only will the right time and circumstances for your speaking be apparent, but you'll know exactly what to say from what Mask.

An important part of Maat Magick is the Dance of the Mask, or Mask-Dancing. You build a collection of Masks, or artificial Egos, to help you establish rapport with any person with whom you are conversing.

One satisfactory method I've found is to base the Mask collection on the Trump cards of the Tarot. In ritual, you first meditate on a card, immerse yourself in its imagery and absorb

as much of its essence as you can. Next, you dance the essence of the card, in full body movement and in mudras, or hand-gestures. The third stage is practice, using the Mask in public circumstances, in conversations.

The meditation-dancing-using rite should be done for each card. It's not necessary to acquire the Masks in the strict order of the Tarot; you could prepare them as needed. The entire set of Masks that you craft will become full-time aspects of your personality, so when need arises, all you need to do is shift emphasis in your consciousness, and you'll be dancing the proper Mask. It would be an interesting experiment if each of you were to choose a different Mask to dance for the next meeting of this class.

To find and use your True Voice, your ma kheru, proceed in a reverse manner compared to the Dance of the Mask. Choose a traditional Word of Power to work with, such as ABRAHADABRA, IAO, OM, or IPSOS, the primary Word of Power in Maat Magick. You can do this outdoors in a solitary location, or you can do it in your temple; find a place where you won't be self-conscious about other people hearing you.

Banish the space, then stand or sit comfortably. Begin by repeating the Word of Power silently in your mind until its vibrations fill your being; whisper the word, then, until it calls to your voice. Begin by saying the Word in a very quiet manner until it tells you to increase the volume. Try keeping your voice in its lower register, where it feels like it originates in your Muladhara Chakra and uses your whole abdomen as the base of its breath. Experiment with pitch and volume until your head and body begin to resonate and vibrate. At any point in this process, from the initial silent repetition to the physical vibration, you may hear and/or feel a roaring sound, somewhat like the sound you hear when you yawn.

Leave a bit of time between soundings of the Word so you can perceive the roar. When you hear it and feel your skull vibrating physically at the same time, you'll know you've found your True

Voice. You will probably be surprised how quiet it actually is, in terms of volume. Make a daily practice of sounding a Word of Power with your ma kheru, and keep notes of what you observe in your Magickal Record. When you are confident about it, try sounding open vowels, then let what syllables and sounds occur to you to find voice. In such a way you may encounter personal Words of Power. You may find your Words in visions or in dreams or in something overheard at random. Whatever the method, preparing your True Voice invites the knowledge of Words of Power.

As a general rule of Magickal practice, never raise power without having a definite place for it to go. If you just turn it loose in the Cosmos, it can feed things you might not care to nourish, or tip a delicate balance in a direction you wouldn't care to live with. Earth your Magickal power in work of one kind or another.

Sit comfortably and close your eyes. Feel yourself in your usual location behind your eyes, a point of consciousness and light.

Look around at the structures in your skull, the neurons and blood vessels and the bony curve of your skull. Move slowly toward the back of your brain, then around and under it to the brain stem and spinal cord. Descend the length of your spinal cord, following its silvery white length through the tunnel of your spine, past all its lateral branchings, until you reach the Muladhara Chakra at the base of your spine.

Enter the radiance of the lotus of light, and enter the firesnake of Kundalini that is curled three and a half times around the Shivalingam in the center of the Chakra lotus. Arouse it to action with your Will, and ride its head as it rises in the spinal channel. As you pass each of the Chakras, set them spinning faster and shining brighter—the Svadhisthana, the Manipura and the Anahata.

We reach the Vishuda Chakra, and the power of Kundalini fills it and sets its lotus of light to spinning. Your throat may

begin to feel warm, with the warmth spreading to your heart and your mouth. Place yourself in the center of the lotus of light and look around you. You are in the center of a vast cavern of crystal where the silence rings with its own echoes. The energy of the Chakra gleams and sparkles from the facets of the dome above and of the walls around you.

You can feel my presence in the cavern with you, as well as the presence of the others in the world who are performing a similar meditation. We are each in our own Vishuda Chakras, yet we are together in the Cosmic Vishuda Chakra, the human Vishuda Chakra, and in the Astral Vishuda Chakra. The worlds are as numerous as echoes, and so are we—reflected in an infinity of crystal faces.

Begin with a long sounding of OM, which you'll sustain until it wants to fade to silence. Then begin sounding the four pronunciations of IPSOS: IPSOS; IPShOS; IPSOSh; IPShOSh.

Your sounding of the Word will echo back to you from all directions; you must listen for the resonance that tells you that you have reached the right pitch, volume and cycle of repetition.

This resonance creates a sphere of silence in its midst. From this silence, continue vibrating the Word until you are filled with pure sound. I suggest that you aim for a quiet intensity.

You will notice, with IPSOS, that the Samekhs (S) and Shins (Sh) produce a hissing sound, like snakes and whispers, or like the universal request for silence. A brief pause between pronunciations creates a window through which silent information can pass.)

OM.... Then: IPSOS—IPShOS—IPSOSh—IPShOSh...

Rise from the center of the Chakra lotus and return to the spinal cord. Extend your vision to the external world from that place, and note what you see in the room and what you see of the furnishings in the room. Move your attention back inside your throat, in the spinal channel, then rise slowly to your skull and

resume your usual place behind your eyes. When you are ready to do so, open your eyes and gently stretch your body.

The Magick of the Word, and the Magick of words, are like Magick in general: they are morally neutral and can be used for good or used for evil. The charismatic attraction of the activated heart Chakra, the Anahata, combined with the True Voice, can be extremely persuasive in convincing other people to believe what you are saying. As you progress along your Initiatory path, you will become ever more aware that all words are only partially true, and therefore partially false, and many times words are totally inadequate to express reality.

The Truth you find in your visions and experiences soon outstrips the ability of language to accurately describe it, and yet you have an obligation to teach and to share your wisdom with the world. The essence of the paradox is well-stated in Crowley's Liber B vel Magi:

"Let Him beware of abstinence from action. For the curse of his grade is that he must speak Truth, that the Falsehood thereof may enslave the souls of men."

Many times, the best way to convey the truths of Initiation is by the Socratic method, where you ask the enquirer questions in such a way that his or her answers provide the truth through internal discovery. Another way to help effectively is to direct the enquirer to perform a certain ritual or exercise that is likely to produce the conditions for enlightenment. Asking yourself the right questions can speed your own spiritual evolution also.

As an assignment, I would like you to write down three questions you could ask yourself that would lead you to find a closer approximation to truth in your outlook on life, on your philosophy. If you find answers in the process, please write them down also. I recommend that you practice sounding Words of Power, keeping in mind that all such Words should be directed in some way toward the manifestation of your Will.

LECTURE 7

Today we will consider the Ajna Chakra, the 'Third Eye, in which is anchored the Forgotten One of Curiosity.

If we review our previous discussions, we can see that the function of each Chakra is based, from a certain point of view, upon the Chakras below it and upon their functions. The Muladhara Chakra, at the base of the spine, establishes our relationship with all living things at the simplest and most basic level.

Hunger provides an organism with fresh energy to replace the energy spent on the processes of life, a replacement supplied by different means in the different Kingdoms of being. In the growth of a crystal in a saturated solution, in the photosynthesis of sunlight, water and nitrogen into carbohydrates and proteins by plants, and in the consumption of plants, other animals, water and minerals by all animals, we find various solutions to meet the needs of Hunger.

Our first step in complexity from this simple, but elegant, beginning is enshrined in the Svadhisthana Chakra and the Forgotten One of sex. When we were one-celled organisms, we were virtually immortal, barring accident and predation. When we swam among abundant food, we would just duplicate our genetic material, our DNA, move the original molecular helix and its replica apart, pinch our cytoplasm into roughly equal masses, grow a new outer membrane for each, and behold—we

were then two where one once swam.

When we became complex and shifted our organizing identity into a collection of specialized cells that united for life, we developed the replication strategy of sex. Of course, as single cells, we would occasionally participate in conjugation with our fellows for the exchange of genetic material, but DNA wanted a richer palette to work with, something that would take its art to a new level of complexity. Sex improved our aesthetic contribution to existence while providing survival insurance; with more variety among its members, a species had a better chance of surviving radical changes in habitat and climate, not to mention a cataclysmic meteor strike here and there.

The major drawback to the invention of sex was the loss of individual immortality; the complexity that brought sex also brought death. It's much more difficult to maintain an elegant collection of specialized cells and tissues against the ravages of gravity, radiation and weather than it is for a single cell to remain fat and happy floating in its watery environment. The stark reality of death inspired the defense of life for oneself and one's kin. We could live on in our children, but we had to concern ourselves with their survival.

The fight or flight instinct extended itself to include the use and possession of lands from which we obtained food, in one way or another, for ourselves and our families, and in which we established dwelling places in which to shelter ourselves from the weather. Our Manipura Chakra functioned so well in this regard that human history has been, for the most part, a history of wars and conquests.

In the heart Chakra, the Anahata, we found a balance for aggression and defense, the Clanning instinct that was, I surmise, the basis for love as we know it today. It, in turn, was most likely based on the emotional bond between mother and child and the bond between mates that arises from sexual attraction.

Whatever its origins, the Clanning urge functions as the social glue which binds our civilizations together, working with

the Forgotten One of flight or fight to shape tribes, nations, and states.

The Forgotten One of the Vishuda Chakra, speech or communication in general, arose for many reasons. Its practical aspects include organizing many people to work on large projects and passing along the accumulated wisdom of the ancestors to the children. Speech also serves to delight the intelligence, the mind and the soul in the arts of oratory, drama, poetry and song.

It is perhaps the silent speech of writing which serves to distinguish us as a genus apart from other mammals on the planet. The written word was the first effective time machine we invented, carrying information to a future beyond the powers of living memory and its survival.

The benefits of the operations of all these Chakras provide the leisure for abstract thinking, for the development of natural philosophy, or what we call Science today, for the refinement of the arts, and for the consideration of metaphysics. The Ajna Chakra is the seat of curiosity. Other species exhibit curiosity, but in humans it combines with our other abilities to produce the life of the mind as we know it today: logical, abstract, often mathematical, and, at the same time, aesthetic, intuitive, and often romantic.

As a survival instinct, curiosity leads to the discovery of new things to eat, new places to live and hunt in, new uses for the natural materials we live with. Curiosity leads to invention, exploration, experiment, and, in some cases, to injury and death.

In general, we have been willing to risk our lives for new knowledge, even when it means defying conventional wisdom and taboo. Even today it's possible to find people who hold that there are things we are not "supposed" to know. The story of Adam and Eve in Eden is one of the more famous stories about forbidden knowledge. If we think about Galileo and Darwin, and their problems with dogmatists, we have strong examples of what might be called anti-curiosity. Magickians must be alert for anti-curiosity manifestations even today in order to avoid

interference with our work. In America, there are Christian fundamentalists who read the Bible in a literal way and take its poetry as statements of fact. They hold that anyone who is not with them is against them, and that those who practice the Occult sciences are agents of Satan. I would like to know if you have anything similar in Europe.

This virulent form of anti-curiosity is a major reason to practice silence and discretion about your Magick. It's better to avoid confrontations with closed minds on the Outer; much more effective are the means we have to bypass the conscious censors with which they guard themselves. These means are the arts and example on the Outer and ritual and Angelic communication on the Inner.

Through subtlety and art we can insinuate questions into the consciousness of those individuals best described in a slogan seen on some American car bumper stickers: "The Bible says it, I believe it, that settles it."

There are also militant atheists who reject the operation of Intelligence and the existence of nonphysical realms in which It operates. These have taken Science for their religion; their minds are often as closed as religionists'. Even though a person may consciously reject data that do not fit his or her preconceived notions, the Ajna still tracks the fascinating ideas and reports to the Unconscious.

It's not the business of the Magickian to provide answers to the big questions of life; each individual has to work them out individually. We do have an obligation, however, to guide people toward asking the right questions and to suggest methods and exercises that will enable them to recognize answers when they see them. In order to do this, we have to honor our Forgotten One of curiosity and pursue truth throughout our own lives, no matter how uncomfortable and/or crazy it makes us.

Maat Magick is named after the principle of Truth for a number of reasons. The original motives, which are based on Aleister Crowley's system of naming the Aeons, are still valid,

but the passage of time has revealed a number of other ways in which the name applies.

As much as the human mind craves absolutes, it is doomed to constant frustration in that regard because there are very few absolutes in life. The one thing in life that we can count on is death; all things born, sprouted, assembled or congealed and set alight from giant gas clouds will, in time, die in one way or another. Everything else in the realm of Duality is uncertain, so we tend to invent absolutes to console ourselves and banish our terrors.

Truth seems to be a fluid thing, a relative thing that changes loyalties and applications as it moves from one level of existence to another. Magick, as the Science and the Art of causing change to occur in conformity with Will, operates in the realm of Dualism, where all things are illusion. The Magus deals in images and imagination; that which we call Reality is, indeed, its own opposite. We're making up everything as we go along, although we generally don't remember the process as we become immersed in the details of life.

It doesn't matter, in practical terms, just how we are or the Universe is; we're here as part of it and part of our being here consists of finding out whatever we can about whatever we can. Our curiosity is a combination of gift and curse from our divine DNA. It not only helps us survive in a changing environment, but curiosity is a gateway to transcending the programming of our genes and our instincts. It's vitally necessary to true mental health and genuine freedom.

It's essential to Maat Magick to develop and exercise our Ajna, and to follow our curiosity wherever it leads us. Exploring those things that capture our attention is part of discovering our True Will and expanding our self-knowledge.

As soon as we are born, we begin to explore the world around us by using our physical senses. As we gain strength and mobility, we range as far as we can in order to see new things, touch and taste unfamiliar objects, and follow intriguing sounds. After we

gain the use of language, we love to hear stories family members tell us, as well as to listen to and watch radio, television, films and recordings. When we learn to read, the world opens up to us in a new way through books.

There are realms of existence beyond the physical senses and the knowledge conveyed by language. We are able to explore these realms by using means of perception that are ordinarily hidden from us; indeed, much of Magick concerns information obtained through the subtler senses and through direct access to the Akashic Record, which is the knowledge of all events in the lives of the many Universes, past, present, future, and alternative.

Most humans have a psychic capacity; usually it goes untrained and only functions sporadically, if at all. One of the best ways to train your Inner senses is the practice of divination, whether by your own method, or through traditional ways, like Tarot reading, palmistry, scrying in a crystal, mirror, or liquid, astrology, runes, etc. First you learn the system and its interpretations, then you practice it intensively on as many people as you can, then pay attention to the hunches and inspirations that come to you before, during and after a reading.

Inspirations, intuitions, feelings and hunches are of varying strengths; sometimes you perceive a fleeting nuance of feeling, sometimes you get a definite piece of information that intrudes upon your other thoughts and won't let go until you do something about it.

Anytime you feel an odd idea, vision or concept, become as still and as silent as you can and focus your attention upon it. Avoid analyzing it at this time, and don't hunt for its source, or criticize the information it brings. The time to test it is later, after you have the whole thing presented to you and after you've written it down or otherwise recorded it.

When you choose a divination system, obtain the material objects, like a deck of Tarot cards, rune stones, black mirror, etc., plus one or more books on the operation of the system.

Practice on yourself on a daily basis. Do a reading for yourself in the morning, and record it in your Magickal Record. At the end of the day write of the successes and failures in your reading; what events materialized or did not materialize that your reading had predicted?

After you have done a number of daily readings for yourself, you'll begin to become familiar with the language of your system, and with what it means in what it says. When you have a working knowledge of your system's language, begin to read for other people for practice. Test yourself by asking your subject to keep his or her major question silently in mind, and see what you can learn about the person and his or her situation just by divination alone. When you've finished the reading and made all the comments you can think of, ask the person how well the reading applied to his or her actual situation. If the person has further questions about the details of what you have read, see if you can provide the answers from the divinatory system. Feel free to draw from your memory and experience also, both in assisting your subject and in assessing the content of the reading.

If you use one or more divination systems frequently, you'll become fluent in your readings. Eventually you'll reach the point where the crystal, the shells or the cards become a means of triggering your direct perception of a person's situation and needs. You might find yourself speaking directly as a channel of information after just a brief time with the physical tools of your system. This direct channeling has a specific psychic aspect to it when it's operating; by replicating the original feeling you have when using the divination system, you will be able to induce the channeling state at will to use in many different situations.

Another way of exercising the Ajna Chakra and developing your psychic abilities is by means of symbols other than those of the Tarot or other divinatory systems. Images we receive in dreams, lucid dreaming or in visionary trance often represent principles or situations beyond their immediate form. Learning to interpret the symbols requires practice, and allowance should

be made for one's own biases in interpretation. There are books in existence that might assist your interpretations, but it's best to discover meanings for yourself. Write down all symbols you receive in your Magickal Record, and look for a consistent pattern of manifestations with which to link them.

You can make Inner vision quests on the Astral planes through techniques similar to the one we use to visit the Chakras as a point of light. Some people find it useful to envision a door marked with a symbol indicating the type of information they seek.

Concentrate on the door's image until you are standing in front of it, then open it and walk through. Whatever you encounter on the other side of the door should have some bearing on what you seek, either directly or in the code of symbols. It's well to check what you see, hear and learn against the tables in Crowley's 777 and in the section titled Sepher Sephiroth.

Always try to confirm information you obtain with your Third Eye by checking its internal consistency and how well the attributes of its form coincide with the traditional colors, metals, godforms, etc. to be found in it.

Also, scrutinize everything you receive from the Astral planes with your own good sense and experience. There are entities dwelling there who delight in deception and confusion, and seek to rob you of your coin of attention and energy. Be wise and skeptical of any information you receive, by means physical and trans-physical.

Your Forgotten One of curiosity sees on the Outer as well as on the inner. Be alert for messages from the universe in the forms of omens and portents encountered in everyday life. It's not uncommon for a person to be frustrated in seeking information about a problem through all the esoteric means we've just mentioned, when the exact, necessary cues and clues arrive by means of overheard conversations, the title of a song that happens to be playing on the radio, in a book picked up and opened at random, and so on.

Such incidents serve to remind us that we are part of a continuum, and that the distinction between Inner and Outer is but a convention of the structure of the human mind.

As we have done in the other lectures, let's visit Kundalini, awaken it to movement, and ride it to the Ajna Chakra. Please sit comfortably and close your eyes. Become aware of your point of consciousness and its surroundings, just a few centimeters behind your eyes. The glow of your awareness and life-force illuminates the densely packed neurons of your brain and the bony vault of your skull. You move from your seat, up and backward, then under your brain to your brainstem and spinal cord.

Now you move down the silver-white cord itself, passing along the tunnel of your vertebrae, down to the branching of nerves near the curve of your coccyx, and into the Muladhara Chakra. Here the firesnake is coiled three and a half times in the fundamental lotus of your body. Enter the Chakra, and project the power of your awareness to set the lotus of light rotating more rapidly and to induce Kundalini to begin its rising. As it stirs, take your place on its head and begin moving upward yourself, drawing the serpent power with you, becoming one with it.

As you pass each Chakra, touch it as Kundalini touches it, setting it spinning more rapidly and with more energy radiating from it.

Pass the Svadhisthana, the Manipura, the Anahata, the Vishuda, then into the Ajna itself. Ah, surprise! This is your familiar place, the usual seat of your consciousness, and now it glows and rotates, a lotus of light into which the light of your point of consciousness blends itself.

Feel your Third Eye opening, and look about you through it. The whole room is suffused with light, everything in it standing out clearly, with the other people in it radiating like beacons.

Yes, this is your familiar home, your base of operations, but how different it seems in its new illumination!

Absorb everything about the new glory of your familiar place. This is how it can be all the time, after a little practice on

a daily basis. Even when you use your physical eyes, the world will appear to you closer to its true self—naive, mysterious, and beautiful.

If you will it to be so, Kundalini can be permanently awake, invigorating all your Chakras, attuning you to the Universe around you, illuminating Truth in all things and in all beings.

The bone of your forehead is now as transparent as crystal, no longer a barrier to your true vision. You can see the physical world around you as well as the nonphysical realms of the Astral, Etheric and Spiritual planes. In its awakened state, charged with Kundalini's serpent power, your Ajna Chakra becomes your Wise Eye, knowing where to look and knowing how to recognize truth.

Certain schools of esoteric teaching advise the Initiate to practice dwelling in this condition during life, for it is from the Ajna that you project your consciousness into the Cosmos on the death of your physical body. The technique consists of withdrawing your life-force from your fingers, toes, arms, legs, and trunk until it's all concentrated in the Ajna; when the right time comes, you take flight as a coherent unit of spiritual energy.

What you do or what becomes of you after physical death is outside the scope of these lectures; based on life experience, however, it makes sense to be as coherent and as integrated as possible. Not all of us have the leisure of a long dying in which to prepare ourselves, so it seems wise to prepare now and maintain your readiness for whenever and however death finds you. Accident, violence, or swift-moving disease can catch any of us unaware.

If we keep the Ajna activated as a matter of habit, and spend a short meditation period each day practicing the gathering of the life-force, we can be ready for anything. To maintain a serene mind in thinking about dying, I recommend greeting each morning when you awaken with the Native American affirmation:

"Today is a good day to die."

As inviting as the prospect of death might be, at times, we will live out the span of our lives just long enough to complete the phase of the Great Work we were born for.

I would like to hear about your results in divination and in your Astral visualizations.

In any case, success to your Work.

LECTURE 8

Welcome to lecture number eight in our series on Maat Magick.

Today we consider the Bindu, which some say isn't a Chakra, but I think that it functions as one in Maat Magick. Originally, I did not consider the Bindu to represent a Forgotten One, or survival urge, but I know now that it does: the Ego, or sense of individual selfhood.

Sigmund Freud first used the term in his psychological philosophy to represent the central, waking self; it was flanked by the Superego and the Id. He saw the Superego's influence as that of the conscience, the Big Parent who controls the behavior of the Ego with rules and restrictions.

The Id is the animal nature of man, the dark, amoral desires suppressed by the imposition of parental and societal dictates. Freud's thinking was focused on sexuality as the source of many psychological ills, a natural assumption in the times that he lived.

The Victorian era in Europe and in the United States was a time of collective hubris, or overweening pride; humanity—especially Caucasian, capitalist /aristocratic humanity—was thought to be the Crown of Creation. During that time, we denied our animal nature through pretense, prudery, and assumed superiority. The African, the Asiatic, the Indian were thought to be closer to animals than the white race was, and hence required the rule of the superior whites in order to improve their morals and their levels of civilization.

This type of thinking justified the invasion and conquest of native peoples and the building of political and economic empires around the world. It also justified the conceit that through uplifting thought we could improve human nature to the point that our animal nature would be under the complete control of rational mind.

The word "Ego" has passed into general use, and is usually taken to mean an inflated sense of self-importance. In our present discussion, Ego is simply the sense of self, the entity we attach to our name. It's the entity that lives behind our eyes, and we usually pay little attention to it once we are fully adult, except on occasions when it registers pain in some form. This pain usually occurs when we are denied the respect we grant to other people, or when someone lies to us or about us, or when someone else abuses the trust we've given them.

In this regard, the Ego can be thought of as a higher echo or octave of the self-preservation instincts. The Ego keeps watch over our status in the group or groups we belong to. It has its roots in the time in our past where status governed eating and mating privileges; the more respect one earned or commanded, the more likely one's genetic heritage would be passed on to healthy offspring.

One could say that our little god DNA tolerates such individual ambition, but only from its own molecular point of view, insofar as the individual ambition serves the species' continuance. The divine DNA cares as much about our individuality as we care about a single sperm cell or a single egg.

Under the influence of Ego, individually and collectively, the human race developed the ideas of honor, vengeance, caste, class, rank and hierarchy. In its most pathetic and ignorant condition, Ego requires someone to look down on, someone to feel superior to.

This condition generates the bully, the snob, the dictator, the elect and the damned. The Ego can also achieve the opposite state of self-deprecation, wherein it makes one feel inferior,

sinful, guilty and desirous of punishment and humiliation. Either state blocks Magickal transformation and can mire one for a long time in stasis and stagnation.

The first step in Initiation and the search for wisdom is defined by two words: "Know thyself."

Maat rules this activity if the course of knowing oneself is sincere. Our Ego can be a problem here since it wants to see itself as already possessing that which we seek. It dislikes our faults and failures and wants to disown them. The only way to know ourselves accurately is through complete, and sometimes painful, honesty.

A useful tool in the course of self-knowledge is to write down on paper your description of a perfect human being. Use this description to assess yourself and your life. Where do you match and where do you miss the mark when you compare yourself to your ideas of human perfection? The next step is to ask your close friends and family members for their honest opinion of you on the points of perfection, as well as on the points that they hold to be important in being human. You have to back such a request with a promise of no reprisal should the other offend your Ego—and then keep that promise.

True humility is the accurate grasp of oneself in terms of strengths and weaknesses, good and evil, success and failure, clarity and confusion. True humility is the only successful means of controlling the Ego, of keeping it in its place and of keeping it in balance. My friend Louis Martinié once said that self-knowledge concerns knowing one's place on the food chain.

By extending the metaphor, we need to know our place in the world, our specific function in life, the mission we accepted when we consented to become flesh and blood.

Our purpose and identity do not necessarily imply reincarnational continuity, although reincarnation, along with the idea of Karma, has been a useful concept in many Initiated traditions. In my own current opinion (and this opinion has changed over the years with the accumulation of experience)

we build our identity, our Ego, from experience as interpreted through our physical senses and our neurological capabilities. Our individuality and identity grow from a combination of heredity and environment until we have achieved a complexity substantial enough to resonate, in the mode we call human, with the divine Intelligence that permeates all of existence.

Contributing to this opinion are accounts of feral children who have been deprived of normal human contact from their infancy, whether through parental neglect, neural disorders, or from being "reared by animals". These people do not use language, nor do they seem able to learn it despite efforts at rehabilitation. They seem healthy enough physically, but, because of a lack of contact and instruction at an early age, remain substantially abnormal. Other individuals with impaired brain function also fail to exhibit the abilities of normal people in terms of taking care of their own basic biological needs, much less in conversing and exhibiting a faculty for complex thought.

On the other hand, our species has produced individuals whom we call geniuses, whose accomplishments in the arts and sciences have advanced our general body of knowledge and understanding, as well as our norms of beauty, by quantum leaps and orders of magnitude.

The genius seems to be more closely attuned than normal people are to the divine Intelligence. This closer attunement seems to be a matter of heredity rather than environment. Heredity in this case means the combination of parental genes in a more-than-usually beneficent way, rather than definite physical lines of single genes or a family history of genius. The genius seems more inclined to seek out information from the environment in order to satisfy his or her need of data, rather than depend on others to provide the information for him or her.

Magick and Initiation hold a compensation for those of us born in the spectrum between subnormal and supernormal. Through the strengthening of disciplines, through the

focussing of attention and intention through ritual, through the establishment of new ways of seeing ourselves and the world around us, we can change ourselves and our environment. These changes bring a more abundant life, an expansion of experience and all that this expansion enables us to do.

One of the aims of Maat Magick is to bring our species into its next level of existence, to transform our norm into that which we now consider genius, and to open and expand communication among us. We are social beings who depend upon each other for the physical means of survival as well as for the life of the mind and the spirit. Paradoxically, the individual Maat Magickian must work and explore in strange territory, as it were, blazing trails of experience into realms where he or she is essentially alone.

There are systems of Initiation that can provide a solid beginning for your explorations, but once you become familiar through experience with the things spoken of by these systems, it's your responsibility to take that which is known further into the Unknown. The primary gateway into the Unknown is the essence of your personhood, and only you can enter. This is why self-knowledge is so important.

What is possible to know about oneself? You can know what gives you pleasure and what gives you pain, to a certain degree. You can know what attracts you and what repels you. You can know the relative state of your health and energies, what your reactions are to certain people, places and things. You can know what your astrological influences are, based on your natal horoscope. You can observe and listen to the effect you have on other people, on animals and on plants. You can know what your mirror image looks like, and your image in photos and on videotape. You can hear your own voice on a tape or disc recorder.

Another pair of useful tools is the writing of descriptions of yourself, both from your own point of view, looking at yourself, and from the point of view of an outside observer. In the realms of manifestation, physical, astral, mental and emotional, you are a presence that interacts with your fellows and your environment.

You can list influences in your life that helped to form your present condition, from your infancy and childhood with your family, your playmates and friends, to your education and the teachers you've had, your enemies, rivals, and groups you've been a part of.

List the commonalities and differences you have with other people you know, with the animal kingdom, and with living things in general. What fantasies do you have about yourself? If you could easily become anything or anyone, who would you be? With what literary characters do you most identify? If you ruled the world and could instantly enforce any decree, what would you order?

Use your imagination to shape a world that would be perfect for you, and note what it tells you about yourself. This is one of the joys of Astral work, since there are no limits on your imaginative faculties. When you have a clear picture of yourself in as many dimensions as you can think of, and have listed the ways in which you can improve yourself, set about implementing these improvements.

Maat Magick has ways of changing your heredity and environment so that you become a Homo veritas individual in your present lifetime.

Many years ago, my Magickal Partner and I visited the Plane of the Unborn and established an informational vibration pattern in the atmosphere of that place. This pattern provided directions to the forming souls who were overseeing the development of their future physical bodies for tweaking a few choice genes into their activated condition.

We already have everything we need, genetically, to achieve the next stage in our evolution. Scientists working on the Human Genome mapping project tell of genetic material that seems to have no known function, and seems to act merely as spacing units for the genes whose functions are known.

Although Nature often exhibits redundancy and oversupply, the genes are not inert. Some of them constitute the difference

between Homo sapiens and Homo veritas, and need but to be activated by an influx of prana in order to exert their influence. Other mysterious genes are instructions for even more advanced evolutionary development (such as those that will enable us to thrive in the near-vacuum environment of space), but Maat Magick modestly concerns itself only with our immediate "sapiens" stage at the present time. Even though it's much easier to activate genes while your physical body is still a zygote, you can do it when you're an adult.

To do this, envision and invoke DNA's double-helix image and clearly state your Will to become Homo veritas. Generate and direct a charge of energy toward the image, acknowledge that it's been accomplished, then end the rite. It would be appropriate to employ Sex Magick in the generation of the charge, since sex is DNA's method of change, but Kundalini in its pure form works as well.

I recommend the visualization of the DNA helix instead of trying to describe or imagine specific genes because most of us are not geneticists, and even geneticists aren't able to identify the genes we want to activate. We rely, in this case, on the intelligence of the molecular level; the genes know who they are.

You will gather from the idea of the Plane of the Unborn that your Ego is not your true Self, although it shares something of the true Self's nature. The true Self can and does exist before individual physical bodies come into existence and develop according to genetic plan. The implications and ramifications of this will open to you as you advance in self-knowledge.

In order to complete your Initiation into the essence of Homo veritas, you must arrange for your environment to work with the newly activated genes. The term 'environment' in this case refers to other people like you, those who can link with you and with each other to form the meta-net of communication and awareness that is the distinguishing characteristic of Homo veritas.

You can do this by paying a new kind of attention to people

in your presence physically, and by Astrally scouting the planet for those at a distance. Internet developments evolve and morph swiftly, and seem to be the physical manifestations of Homo v.

The attention you give to those in your presence is quite similar to, if not identical with, the state of mind you acquire while doing a divination. Reserve enough of your mind to comprehend any conversation the other person is having with you, but devote most of it to watching facial expressions, body language, and aura, while observing the tone of voice, what's being said under the words, and what's being avoided. Open yourself to the other person's essence, maintaining an inner silence all the while.

The effect is like "seeing double", or having two pictures of the person superimposed on each other. Many times, the Astral double reveals what the physical presence conceals. What sorts of revelations you share or action you take with each person is a matter of your own judgement.

People who are functioning in the state of Double Consciousness, and those who are on the brink of change will probably be aware of your observation and might well initiate conversation about it with you. Others will need varying amounts of preparatory work. You can plant seeds in their consciousness with questions of the "Have you ever thought about....?" variety.

It's usually wise to avoid giving advice unless you've been requested to do so. There are still other people who are so fixated on themselves, or so weighed down with problems, or who have chosen to remain at an early stage of Inner growth, that you would be wasting your time in a direct approach to species change.

With these latter types, and with people you've not yet met, I suggest that you contact their human essence through the Metaperson of our species. This entity is our future collective self, who, through a type of time travel into its past, gave me the essential ingredients of Maat Magick which is designed to bring itself into existence in our present. There are other people who

have been touched and inspired by this entity, and who know it by other names, or by no name at all.

With me, it calls itself N'Aton, and stands in relation to individual humans as each of us stand in relation to the cells, tissues, and organs of our body. It is the next level of sentient organization of life on planet Earth.

From another point of view, N'Aton is Jung's Racial Unconscious awakened, somewhat matured, and functioning. From a third point of view, N'Aton is a very large cyborg, a cybernetic organism arising through, and keeping in touch with, itself. We participate in this cybernetic organism, in part, by means of the communications technology we see growing around us day by day.

Our essential connection in N'Aton is biology-based telepathy and empathy. We don't absolutely depend upon manufactured hardware in order to establish this connection in the physical plane.

The development of our collective self, our Metaperson, depends upon neither mindless conformity to the will of the majority, nor upon a total dependence on the telepathic connection for individual well being. The more diverse, odd and eccentric we are as individuals, the richer, deeper, more understanding and wiser N'Aton becomes.

In the Thelemic system of Aeons and their functions, the Aeon of Horus, began in 1904 with the writing of Liber AL vel Legis, aimed at destroying the remnants of the Aeon of Osiris which preceded it.

We are recognizing the evil results of ancestral attitudes that have caused widespread misuse of the environment. We are working to correct the sins of the past, such as strip mining, clearcut logging, slash and burn agriculture, overgrazing of grasslands and overfishing of oceans, lakes and streams. We are cleaning up polluted air, water and earth, and looking for ways to safely dispose of nuclear waste and toxic chemicals.

In our public and political mode, at least, many of us have

renounced wars of conquest and subjugation, colonizing, slavery, torture and forced labor. Although the work has just begun in the area of securing human rights for all members of our species, official recognition of the necessity of doing so gives weight, or gravitas, to the continuing of the process.

We have only begun restoring things our ancestors have despoiled; we have only begun to assume the responsibilities of a maturing species. Many of us are still out of tune with Nature, self and each other; the work of awakening the soul of humanity lies before us.

I want to conclude this lecture with our usual Inner visit with Kundalini; you will notice that the method for bringing the firesnake to the Bindu is different from our previous experiences.

Sit comfortably and close your eyes. Let your breathing become deep and regular; when the time is right, sound three OMs.

Become aware of your center of consciousness in its usual place, a few centimeters behind your eyes. This center is radiating energy as a glowing light, illuminating the interconnected neurons of your brain, the blood vessels bringing nourishment and taking away waste, the white vault of your skull. Remember all the journeys you've taken down your spine to draw the Kundalini up to and through each Chakra. Recall your encounters with your Chakras: the Muladhara, the Svadhisthana, Manipura, Anahata, Vishuda, and Ajna.

Through the nerve connections, feel each Chakra spinning and glowing, pulsing with its unique frequency of energy. Hover in the region where the brainstem joins the brain and call Kundalini to you. Feel the energy stir at the base of your spine, heeding your call and your desire for it. You feel it rushing up the channel of your vertebrae like a train in a tunnel, approaching you at high speed and with intense energy.

Open yourself wide and let the fire take you, electrifying you, exploding you into a million suns and galaxies, expanding you to contain the Cosmos. Within you burn the countless stars,

glowing nebulae, and quasars; within you roll huge gravities, neutron stars and black holes. For Aeons, you contemplate all this glory you contain, marveling at supernovas, photon storms, neutrino gales, riding the expansion and attenuation of all manifestation.

Gradually, you become aware of a connection that gently pulls you in a direction that seems below and before you. You notice that you inhabit a body of light, shaped as your usual form, but with an umbilicus of energy attached to it. As you sense your movement with the cord, you become aware of being contained by the Cosmos while at the same time you contain it. It's as though you were Janus, facing in opposite directions and seeing the same view in both of them.

The darkness and brilliance of interstellar space fades as you find yourself once more in the bone Temple of your skull. (I am reminded here that in Maat Magick's Word of Power, IPSOS, the word OS means both mouth and bone.) Across the folded surface of your cerebrum flicker the electric traces of thought, flashing through rainbow colors, appearing and disappearing in waves and tides.

The pituitary gland, the body's Alchemist, sends its commands through the blood to the other glands to produce your Elixir of Life. Your pineal body, old lizard's eye, awaits your return like a throne vacated by a monarch. As you settle into your usual place behind your eyes, you become aware of a background sound, a great changing chord with countless notes, from the song of hydrogen that permeates interstellar space to the hum of living minds around you, human and otherwise.

The chord doesn't occupy your attention, but surrounds your attention in a sense of completion. You find yourself sounding your own silent notes, blending your essence into the harmony. The sense of your physical body returns, strong, rested, and filled with the energy of prana/Kundalini. You feel your Chakras spinning, each at its proper rate, glowing with radiating power.

Your sense of self has changed; it's vast, calm, containing your

body instead of being contained by it. You become aware of new memories, memories that your individuality hasn't experienced before, but real, vivid, manyfold. You feel a multitude of loves and hates, desires and guilts, prides and fears. You feel like a giant, sitting on a mountain instead of in a room, able to span continents and oceans in a few strides.

Move your fingers gently; you return to your physical body's true dimensions, its true location. Gently, slowly, roll your head clockwise, then in the other direction. Follow your breathing, then increase the amount of air you take with each breath. Gently, slowly, open your eyes and stretch your muscles.

You can repeat this journey in your own Temple at any time. It's a useful antidote to depression and fatigue, emotional strain and spiritual dryness. Practice dwelling in your expanded state during your daily activities and usual occupations. Watch your Ego, your sense of individuality, from "outside" in stressful situations and when dealing with difficult people. Contemplate the task of awakening the human race into its Double Consciousness; in the expanded state, you'll sense where and when to exert the power of your Magick.

LECTURE 9

elcome to the ninth lecture in our series on Maat Magick. Today we consider the Supreme Chakra, the Sahasrara, and its Forgotten One, God-hunger. I had considered calling this urge the Religious Impulse, but the term God-hunger is closer to its reality.

God-hunger arises from our nature, from our senses, from our mind, from our ability to respond in feeling and action to the world around us. God-hunger begins in our responses to the beauty of a sunset after a storm, to the vastness of the night sky, to the loveliness of a spider's web full of dew at dawn. It originates in fear and terror of tornados, earthquakes, volcanos, and other dangers of a planet full of life, water and moving tectonic plates.

We hope for and fear the existence of a being or beings larger, wiser and more powerful than we are in the face of death and its awe-giving mystery.

We see a life of the spirit in the intangible actions we perform every day, such as dreaming, thinking, and imagining; we see it as an unseen agency that is responsible for unlikely occurrences, as an explanation for events for which we see no cause. In the experience of injustice as we feel it, injustice of illness, loss, and harmful actions of our fellow humans, we invent the concepts of Fate, of Kismet, of Karma, of heaven and hell, of God's mysterious ways.

We reason that the world we see around us must have had an origin at the beginning of time, and since, in our experience,

every effect has a cause or causes, that which caused the universe must be larger and more powerful than is the universe itself.

Science has unveiled many mysteries in its short existence, but there seem to be questions that remain unanswered—perhaps not because they are unanswerable, but because we haven't yet asked the questions in the right manner.

Organized religions have prospered through the ages because they promise to fill the God-hunger. Unfortunately, they substitute doctrine, commandments and ritual for the direct experience for which all human souls yearn.

When the experience is not forthcoming, organized religions fall back on a promise of heavenly reward after death. The concept of sin, on the other hand, threatens eternal punishment, so the religion has both the carrot and the stick with which to control the actions and beliefs of the faithful. Since both consequences are scheduled to happen after death, there are no dissatisfied customers to complain of fraud, nor satisfied members of the flock to testify about the accuracy of the claims.

The various Holy Books are written by people claiming Divine inspiration; certain portions of them have been touched by extraordinary thinking and feeling, but all of them have been written, revised, copied and translated by human beings with their own moral, social and philosophical agendas. The clergy of various faiths add their own interpretations to the words of the Holy Books, then preach to the faithful the meanings and lessons to be taken from the words.

The faithful of the various religions are encouraged to accept the words of the clergy, traditional forms of worship, and whatever the doctrines and dogmas have to say about the nature of the Divine, about human nature, and about the realities of human life. For the vast majority of the faithful, all this suffices to convince them that their God-hunger is being met by the emotional essence of religion. Even those who attain ecstasy in charismatic services experience it in terms of their religious tenets and concepts.

Let us examine this Forgotten One of God-hunger. Why can, or should, it be called a forgotten one, when the religious impulse has shaped history through wars, pogroms, crusades, inquisitions, conquests, forced conversions and the economic exploitation of native peoples? Even in the present, religion is invoked to justify restrictive legislation and abrogated rights, genital mutilation and male domination.

To be fair, religion has also inspired great art in architecture, sculpture, painting and music, even though some religions forbid 'graven images'. There have been saints who have transcended their ordinary consciousness through religion, and religious-based charities, schools and hospitals have contributed to the well-being of humankind.

God-hunger is forgotten, in the main, precisely because of religion. We are social animals, much like our cousins the apes and chimpanzees. We choose leaders from among us to make decisions for group behavior and action, and also to take personal risks, as heros, for the group on some occasions.

In the Aeon of Isis, the Hero-King was wed, symbolically, to the Earth or to the place goddess of the group's land or territory in hieros gamos, or sacred marriage. When the King grew old or ill, or when the food supply failed, the old King was slain and a new King was appointed in his place. The new King rejuvenated the goddess and the natural world, which was her expression, thus invigorating and renewing the food supply.

Some say that in the Aeon of Osiris, the God-King assumed sole authority and absolute rule. The female force was subjugated, as were the women who embodied it. Historically, in some societies, fathers had the power of life and death over their children. Even in Christianity, the person sacrificed is the Son, while the Father, whose essence demands the sacrifice, abides in the safety and comfort of heaven.

Western theology teaches that Man is made in the image and likeness of god; Western Magick teaches that that which is below is like that which is above, and that which is above is like

that which is below. The invention and transmission of Western religious doctrine created images of the Divine Intelligence using templates of human behavior that were far from the finest or most admirable of our qualities.

The Biblical God admits to being jealous, and the story of Eden and the fall of Adam and Eve is a story of entrapment.

The Book of Job has God betting the Adversary that Job's loyalty can withstand any misfortune. He then visits pain and loss upon that poor human as a test, pain and loss unearned by Job's deeds. In the New Testament, God requires his own death, in the person of the Son, as a redemption for human sin; given the quality of omnipotence that doctrine ascribes to him, one can only conclude that the God of the Bible enjoys pain, suffering and death. In a human, such enjoyment would be considered psychopathic.

That the worship of such a deity could not prevent true mystics from arising from among the faithful, mystics like John of the Cross and Teresa of Avila, demonstrates that the gates to direct experience of Divine Intelligence cannot be blocked, even though they are obscured.

Maat Magick, like any true, personally transformative Magick, suggests methods whereby you can bypass the traditional explanations of why things are the way they are, and discover Truth for yourself.

Pierre Tielhard de Chardin, Jesuit priest and paleontologist, states "Everything that rises must converge".

This is as true of Initiatory attainment as it is of human society and collective accomplishment. Our exploration of Kundalini, the Chakras, and the Forgotten Ones has been a recapitulation of our individual and species development from our prehuman origins to the present day. As Kundalini rises in our spine, our survival history manifests in our awareness, converging, if all goes well, in knowledge of our True Self.

What is the human individual? We are each a living organism of limited independence, comprised of many cells, each of which

is a living organism of even more limited independence. Our cells are being born and dying throughout our lives, replacing each other in the specialized tissues, organs, bone and muscle that comprise our physical bodies.

It is usual to consider our individuality bounded by our skin, separate from other individuals, unique, irreplaceable, whole and self-aware. When we immerse our awareness in our individuality, we often feel alienated, adrift, and disconnected from our fellow humans and other living creatures.

In the press of city living, we can feel lost in a crowd; in working for a corporation or a bureaucracy, we can feel like cogs in a machine. On the other hand, at a sports event, a concert, a parade, or on a crowded dance floor, we can feel part of an organic whole, united with those around us in a common focus, experience or action. Perhaps the reality of our individuality isn't as hard-edged as we think it is.

The cells of our body depend upon each other for nourishment and instructions, but blood transfusions and organ transplants show that they can live in environments other than their native sites.

Our skin merges with its surroundings as epidermal cells die and flake off; the barber sweeps up our hair and sends it to a landfill. The water in our cells has passed through millions of spiracles and kidneys, and the air we breathe has journeyed through billions of leaves and lungs. Our food, once living vegetable, animal, and mineral entities, provides our cells with the chemicals needed for self-construction. When we die, our chemicals will be released, in turn, to feed other living things.

Our individuality, then, is a temporary configuration of chemicals organized into cell-based structures that support our intelligence, awareness, and continuity. The DNA molecule that determines our form and functions manifests in the physical realm as a code built into a strand of chemicals, carrying meaning like the knotted strings of primitive societies carried messages.

On the astral level of being, the code looks like us. In Western

esoteric tradition, the physical world we know through our senses is the end product of a chain of conditions and events that constitute the autobiography of light. It appears to our senses, and to the mind connected to them, that the physical world generates the worlds of dream, thought, feeling, and spirit. Both views are correct.

Nature as we know it arose from the accumulated density of energy and matter, both as a product of the Big Bang, and as an idea of the Divine Intelligence. Science describes the sequences of natural processes, not the meanings of them.

Through observation, analysis, speculation, experiment and prediction, scientists collect descriptive truths about humans and our universe. If you maintain a layperson's interest in the advances of science, and then cover a number of different scientific fields, it's possible to notice a pattern that hints of an organizing principle of all phenomena.   I consider this organizing principle to be the shadow of God, the aesthetics of Divine Intelligence.

As part of Nature, as part of phenomena, we humans are shaped by this same organizing principle. As such, we can be said to be made in the image and likeness of God.

Where religion and religious art have failed to render the truth is in making the gods or God look like people, and in assigning to them, or to It, human characteristics. In the major Western religions, God is male. We fail to realize that our human gender and sexual arrangement is particular to our planet and that humanizing the Divine limits it and our ability to understand it.

We have, then, our sense of individuality and our anthropomorphic image of the Divine Intelligence at the beginning of our quest for the satisfaction of God-hunger. Magick may begin with conventional religious imagery as a preliminary vocabulary of mystical experience, but with a persistent practice, such limitations drop away naturally.

In this lecture series, we've meditated upon and experienced

the energies of each of the major Chakras, in ascending order. The ascending motion is the essence of mysticism, a pursuit of reality in its ever more simple forms, penetrating the illusion of solidity and complexity. We've accompanied Kundalini, the fire-snake of spinal energy, up through the Chakras, from tail to head.

The Sahasrara Chakra above the top of the skull is the place where Kundalini meets the prana of the Universe, merging our life force with the vast tides around us, our planet, our sun, our galaxy, and beyond.

Even with dissolution into the whole of physical, astral and spiritual reality, even with the disappearance of our selves in the experience, while we live we are anchored to the illusion of ourselves in the world. As Magickians, we are conduits, like Prometheus' hollow wand of fire, through which the essence of Divine Intelligence, which is Truth, can be brought back to earth and shared among our fellow humans. It is our duty to conduct the Truth wisely and well, to manifest it in our words, our actions, our support and opposition to the events of our times, our advice to fellow seekers and in our rites of Magick.

The most accurate piece of writing on the reality of the consciousness of the Sahasrara Chakra is the Tao Teh King by Lao Tze. The Tao is beyond description or mental comprehension; one can only experience it. Silence on all levels of existence is necessary in order to perceive Tao. When you experience the silence of the Sahasrara Chakra, you become Tao. You become your very own self on the boundary of the Sephira Kether and the veils of negative existence in which the Tree of Life manifests.

It's impossible to draw up a schedule for any individual's Initiation; some of us take years to overcome defects that delay our progress on the Path, and others of us crash and burn after a brilliant beginning. We, who persevere in our practices and keep a mind open to new data and to our own lacks and areas of ignorance, can attain the state where 'attainment' becomes meaningless. There's not much else to say about the Sahasrara

Chakra, except that it is our link to the rest of the universe on the plane of pure energy, and that its activation marks an important stage of metaphysical maturity.

In this final stage of our Kundalini voyage, we will take the firesnake to its fullest extension, as best we can, and unite with the universal energy that is flowing around us and through us constantly. When we reach the Crown Chakra, chant the words OM and IPSOS alternately until you know and feel the chant is complete.

Sit comfortably and close your eyes. Let your breathing become slow and steady, and become aware of your essence seated in your Bindu and Ajna Chakras. Extend your awareness down your spine, imparting energy to each Chakra in sequence.

Your throat, your heart, your navel, your genitals and your anus all feel the surge of the energy of your attention; their lotuses increase their glow and the speed of their rotation. In your Muladhara Chakra, Kundalini stirs at the touch of your attention.

The central channel of the Sushumna is wide open and free of obstructions. Direct all the energy you feel to the serpent image at the base of your spine, desiring its rising with single-minded concentration. As you inhale, prana fills your lungs and suffuses your body; as you inhale, you draw in cosmic energy through the top of your skull. As you exhale, Kundalini rises like a rocket to meet and mix with the cosmic energy surrounding you and penetrating your brain from above.

With every breath, your firesnake rises to your Sahasrara, gaining more power with each pulsation, until it fountains up in a shower of sparks and stars. A pillar of flame rushes from the top of your head, becoming the fire of stars and galaxies. All of your bodies and systems are a conduit of fantastic power. In the passage of the brilliance that runs through you, you become translucent, then transparent, then gone.

At this point, be silent for a while, then begin intoning OM and IPSOS very softly and slowly. Take the tone of the chant

up the scale until an octave is complete. Bring the chanting to a close when you feel it being solidly earthed.

This is all there is to the ninth lecture. Lecture ten will be a discussion forum, in which we will share our experiences and conclusions about the course. Take some time to reorient yourself to everyday reality. Practice the Kundalini visualization every day, until it becomes a habit for you to be in the state of total openness that it brings.

LECTURE 10

This is our final lecture on Maat Magick, Kundalini, and the Forgotten Ones.

Dr. Naskov has asked me to provide ten questions for the course, and this lecture seems a good time to ask them. I would like to use the questions as a means of establishing the material in the course more firmly in your memories.

1. What do you need on the physical plane for the practice of Magick?

2. Name three activities in Magick that are done primarily on the Astral Planes.

3. What are Mind's proper duties and functions in Magick?

4. How would you describe the relationships between Love and Sex Magick?

5. What is the Holy Guardian Angel?

6. How are Magickal Workings empowered so that the aims of the Working are manifested?

7. In what ways would you improve the Universe?

8. What is your opinion of death?

9. In what ways can you use a Word of Power?

10. What are you? (What else are you?)

Thank you for your interest in Maat Magick.

The three major stages in a Magickian's life are those of Initiate, Adept, and Priest. The High Art is the work of a lifetime, and no matter what stage you are in, you are contributing to the fate of the world.

Magick is a vocation in the same sense that being a doctor, a nun, or a parent is a vocation, or calling, to a way of life. The call to Magick exists everywhere, all the time; the number of people able to hear and to respond to that call seems to be increasing with time. Your calling is your True Will; do that and none shall say nay.

I hope the exercises we performed in touring the Chakras, as well as the theory and practice of Maat Magick, prove useful to you.

Success to your Work.

For further information about Maat Magick and about Magick in general, go to:

BlackMoonPublishing.com

HorusMaatLodge.com

HorusMaat.com/silverstar/

Additional Manuscripts

N'ATON AND I

Ain — Nothing

In 2005, the Horus Maat Lodge year's work was our manifesting N'Aton. I thought it would be useful to our purpose to know and understand this entity as well as possible during the three preparatory months. To this end, I begin with a summary of events and impressions of N'Aton, and some ritual suggestions.

The first time I met N'Aton in 1973, I saw an absence, a person-shaped silhouette of shifting colored shadows. There was no gesture or change of posture to indicate that this entity had noticed me; it felt like I was seeing its back. Although it looked like an absence, it felt like a presence.

Returning from the/a deep past in a group time-travel working, I sensed an extra person among us, one who had not been present at the beginning of the rite. Two other ritualists were aware of our guest. Their confirmation of my perceptions convinced me to keep an open mind in silence.

The second time I saw N'Aton, s/he was no longer a shadow. S/he was a four-dimensional human androgyne/gynander, with skin, hair, and eyes of gold. N'Aton's left side is lit strongly and gleams almost metallically. Hir right side is in deep shadow, a shadow that contains different images on different occasions.

Sometimes N'Aton wears a cloak, sometimes s/he appears naked. The background has been either deep space or an alien landscape.

Usually, hir image has been static, more of a talking head than anything else. Recently, however, N'Aton had begun to dance rather than speak. I was surprised— after all these years — to find the side lighting was not from an off-stage spotlight, but emanates internally. The shadow side generates its own darkness.

Such an image is a mask, an icon, an avatar, shaped mostly (but not totally) from one's own memory and imagination. A visual apprehension isn't necessary to reception of information. Those who do experience a vision more likely than not would see someone or something completely different from what I see. The entity who told me its name is "N'Aton" would probably use a different name with each person s/he meets, according to what seed-sound resonates best with the hearer. Perhaps no name will be given at all. For convenience, I'll continue to use "N'Aton" to mean the representative personality of Homo veritas, humanity's collective consciousness.

A flat mirror, for hand or wall, is needed for part of the working.

Structure your rite as you will, using your accustomed practices as framework. For my own statement of intent, I plan to say "It is my Will to understand more of the entity now known as N'Aton".

At the appropriate time, bring your face and the mirror close together, adjusting the distance until you see a single eye. You may have to deliberately let go of your binocular focus so that both eyes are looking straight ahead.

As you gaze into the eye, talk to N'Aton. Know that you address the future of humanity in our collective consciousness and unconsciousness. Know that we're becoming more aware of each other through our media and our compassion (e.g. a global tsunami response). Consider that you are a vital and unique expediter of our general awakening into double consciousness.

Stop and be still. Look long and deeply into the eye, and expect nothing.

When the time is right, conclude your ritual and write up your report while still in the mind frame of the mirror gazing.

If you have other intentions to energize (personal, global, etc.) it might be more effective to do so before or after the mirror gazing instead of during it.

Repeat the mirror gazing as often as feasible during the following month. There may come a time when you can enter the open-minded silence without using the mirror; feel free to proceed without it when appropriate.

Comments would be appreciated.

Thank you.

AIN Nothing before the beginning and after the end OM

Every event is an encounter by God with your soul.

This post originally appeared on the Horus Maat Lodge e-list in 2005.

MAAT MAGICK &
CHAOS MAGICK

Even though I had read Peter Carroll's *Liber Null and Psychonaut* many years ago, I had never resonated with Chaos Magick as he had presented it. Since discovering the Internet, however, I have met a number of Chaos Magickians online; one of them, Joseph Max of California, published the text of a lecture he had delivered to a Magickal gathering. In it, he cited Maat Magick as a good example of Chaos Magick. It immediately occurred to me to investigate further, to compare and contrast the two methods.

At this point it would be wise to distinguish between the Magickal methods as they appear in print and the individual Mages who use them. Both Chaos Magickians and Maat Magickians tend to be highly individualistic (as is proper in this Art), and every one I have met thus far has his or her own grasp of the methods employed. The Magickians are more similar in their independent creativity than they are different in their philosophy or terminology. I base my statements on how the two methods appear in print, modified by experience and comments from practitioners.

With the exception of Austin Osman Spare's work, there was little, if any, innovation in the field of Western Magick from the death of Aleister Crowley until the early 1970s. Jack Parson's work is firmly Thelemic, distinguished by his passion for freedom and self-sovereignty and by his devotion to the manifestation of Babalon. Charles Stansfeld Jones declared the beginning of

the Aeon of Maat, but failed to develop an initiatory system based on that 'new' frequency of the Magickal Current. Kenneth Grant's explorations of the Nightside of Magick first manifested in print with his *Cults of the Shadow* in 1975 and continues to this day; I see little mention of his work in the literature of Chaos Magick, save as the person who made public the life and works of Spare.

The most obvious similarity between Chaos Magick and Maat Magick is that they are both post-Crowleyan Magicks. Science, technology and global communications have altered the world radically since the end of World War II. Both methods avail themselves of these sources of new metaphor in their general world-views, terminology, and techniques. Chaos Magick declares itself new, and Maat Magick honors its roots, but as Mr. Max points out:

Yes, CM [Chaos Magick] is a 'new' tradition (isn't that an oxymoron?), but as it is based upon deconstruction of the traditional forms, it definitely owes a debt to the past. So I would say that CM is derived from older traditions by deconstruction, whereas MM [Maat Magick] is derived by extrapolation.

The differences in the similarities between the two Magicks is mirrored by the similarities in the differences, as will become clear in the course of our considerations.

Both Magicks have an Aeonic map. In *Liber Kaos*, Mr. Carroll presents a table summarizing his view of the course of past, present and future psychohistory. It uses four Aeons (Shamanic, Religious, Rationalist and Pandemonic) divided into two sub-Aeons each (Animist/Spiritist, Pagan/Monotheist, Atheist/Nihilist, and Chaoist/?) These are presented left-to-right, and above them twine three sine-waves representing the Materialistic Paradigm, the Magickal Paradigm and the Transcendental Paradigm. The waveforms show the relative dominance of each paradigm (the consensus-reality or Zeitgeist of a contemporary culture at any given point in history) for each Aeon and sub-Aeon.

It is an elegant schema, and I commend it to your attention. I have no idea whether any other Chaote subscribes to it or not, but for me it has the satisfying 'click' of a complex idea that makes sense. Maat Magick's Aeonic Map consists of the Nameless Aeon (prehistory-hunting/gathering: animism, shamanism, Voodoo); the Aeon of Isis (herding, farming, fishing: the Great Mother and pagan pantheons); the Aeon of Osiris (city-states, invasion, war: Judaism, Christianity, Islam); the Aeon of Horus (atomic energy, radio, television: Thelema, atheism, existentialism); the Aeon of Maat (string theory, genetic manipulation, the Internet: Chaos Magick, Maat Magick, a growing number of new Magickal methods/schools); and the Wordless Aeon (the near and far manifested future wherein a new species emerges from the human genus).

The Wordless Aeon and the Pandemonic Aeon seem to represent the same 'condition'; the Chaos view sees it as a time when Magick prevails as a way of life, and the Maatian view is of a double state of consciousness, individual and collective. Both Magicks see the manifest future as fundamentally different from the present, on a global scale, and both see the development and use of technology as integral to that difference.

(Note: In the course of developing and using Maat Magick, I have met the 'personality' of our double-consciousnessed future self, who called itself N'Aton. I recognize in the Internet the skeleton and nervous system of N'Aton, 'fleshing-up' even as we speak.)

A sub-similarity exists between the Magicks, in that the Magickal formulae of all Aeons are currently available for competent and appropriate use. I encountered this realization in the course of working with Maat Magick, and called it PanAeonic Magick. Somewhere in the world today there are people practicing and living under the influence of each of the Aeons. Instead of the linear, or even the cumulative, model of the development of Magickal vision and practice, I think the timeless/eternal model most closely approximates 'reality'. The

writings I have seen on Chaos Magick encourage the open and free use of metaphors and techniques of all cultures and ages.

Chaos and Maat Magicks both make use of A.O.Spare's sigil Magick, the process where one's intention is written, reduced, and rearranged into an abstraction on paper (or other suitable material), forgotten, then recalled at a moment of high passion and released into the universe to manifest. The sigilization process moves the intention from conscious awareness to the Unconscious - or, more accurately in my opinion, to the Deep Mind, a phrase used by Jan Fries (*Visual Magick, Helrunar*). This is done in the act of forgetting. The Deep Mind, consisting as it does of the powers accumulated in the course of our evolution from single cells, as well as the underlying connection of all things, can and does act without the restrictions imposed by consciousness and ego. Turning a coherent written sentence into an incomprehensible abstract design removes the intent from the grasp of ordinary consciousness and delivers it to the pre/post-verbal realm of the Deep Mind.

Chaos Magick and Maat Magick also share Spare's use of belief as a tool. Humans tend to be restricted by belief, kept to a specific doctrine or set of dogmas, and provided with a pseudo-security in that restriction. There's a slogan sometimes seen on American bumper-stickers that reads: "The Bible says it, I believe it, and that settles it!". Wars have been fought over differing religious beliefs (Crusades, Jihads and pogroms) as well as over differing philosophies of ethics and/or biology (as in the American Civil War over slavery).

I see belief as an extension of our survival urge of fight or flight, a reflex of grasping tightly the nearest bough when wind disturbs the treetops. Belief must be emptied of content to be an effective Magickal tool, however. One must believe intensely and passionately in the godform one is invoking, for instance, or the transformation of the Magickian into the god will not occur. It is necessary to be able to return to your usual self after the ritual, without that god residing permanently in your belief,

so that when you need to believe in something else on another occasion, you will have a clean, receptive tool available.

The number eight plays a prominent part in both Chaos Magick and Maat Magick. Eight arrows radiating from a central point is the primary symbol of Chaos, and it is used in Liber Kaos as the schema for eight types of Magick that are ascribed to various colors:

Black: Death Magick, for experiencing the nature of death personally, or for sending death-spells. (I refrain from comment.) It seems to resonate with Saturn.

Blue: Wealth Magick is Jupiterian.

Green: Love Magick reflects the nature of Venus.

Yellow: Ego Magick fits with Solar energy. A sub-similarity exists here with Maat Magick's Dance of the Masks.

Purple or Silver: Sex Magick. Purple is for passion, and silver is for the moon.

Orange: Thinking Magick is Mercurial in nature.

Red: War Magick

Octarine: Pure Magick, with octarine being the color which the individual associates with the essence of Magick.

It is interesting to note that although Chaos Magick doesn't use the Tree of Life as a structure template, the colors listed above with their particular Magicks correspond with the Queen Scale colors of the Sephiroth which share the same attributes. For me, Octarine evokes a spinning triad of white, gray and black, the Queen Scale colors of Kether, Chokmah and Binah.

Maat Magick has an eight-fold banishment, and the Forgotten Ones, or survival-urges, are linked to the seven-Chakras-plus-Bindu in an octet.

Other similarities that bear investigation include the construction of an astral temple in one's private 'vestibule' outside the Astral Commons; the probability worlds and the Akasha; and the human origins of gods and their attainment of independent life through generations of worship and belief. There are other similarities which I find each time I read through any of the Chaos literature, and I invite your own investigations.

I found fewer differences than similarities between the two schools, and the first one reflects the 'cussedness' of human nature to an amusing degree.

In writing and speaking about Maat Magick, I have taken great pains to emphasize that it doesn't support the founding of any order, coven or official group of practitioners. The reason for this is simple and basic: Maat Magick, like any valid system of Initiation, self-destructs upon successful completion. It works itself out of a job. What does remain is a network of colleagues who share information about current projects and adventures, help each other out with leads for research and recommended reading, and occasionally congregate for ritual. The latter is quite an undertaking, since the network of Maat Magickians is international and spread out over the USA and elsewhere at flying distances.

Maat Magickians are usually steeped in their own styles of Magickal work of varying kinds, and rarely identify themselves primarily as 'Maat Magickians'. I consider this a healthy indication that the mojo is working as it should.

Despite this basic spirit of disestablishmentarianism, there does exist (mainly on the Astral and online) the Horus-Maat Lodge, whose purpose is to spread the word about the Double Current of Horus and Maat. Since its foundation, the recognition of the existence of PanAeonic Magick seems to have expanded its scope. It was not my idea, but the people who

wanted the Lodge to exist won my cooperation in its founding through their collective charisma, energy, and good intentions. The Lodge's only addresses are www.horusmaat.com and its mailing list; otherwise, there are no meetings, no dues, no tax-free status, no officials, no grades.

Chaos Magick, on the other hand, has the Illuminates of Thanateros (I.O.T). For a complete description, see Mr. Carroll's *Liber Kaos, Appendix 4, 'Liber Pactionis'.*

Mr. Max writes:

"Ouch! Them's fightin' words in some circles! There are far more learned and powerful magicians who have been excommunicated from the IOT than there are currently in their membership! IMNSHO [in my not so humble opinion], the IOT gave up all rights and claims to being the avatars of CM when they decided to become a junior-OTO institute invitation-only degree systems, place all administrative power in one person's hands and declare 'magical war' on anybody they didn't like. The founders Ray Sherwin and even Peter Carroll long ago left in disgust.

"Now there can be made a case for the concept that the IOT is not 'The Pact', but that The Pact is only the 'outer order' and the real IOT is itself like the "invisible A\A\" - to practice Chaos Magic is to be an Illuminate of Thanateros, and 'membership' in any organization is not a requirement. This is how I like to think of it, and it is more in keeping with the original conception of Sherwin and Carroll."

Another distinction I see is that Chaos Magick uses 'servitors' while Maat Magick doesn't. Servitors are entities created, summoned, or obtained to carry out the Magickian's intent by proxy as an automatic device. Maat Magick tends to work through direct impression of intent on the Magickal Current, or 'the ongoingness of things', through which the intent acquires

power to manifest.

Mr. Max:

"Indeed, Chaotes generally are very much into using servitors, but there are many workings that fall into the 'enchantment' category as well. I would not extrapolate a general tendency into a strict 'law'. Most of the work I do is not servitor based ..."

The only other major distinction between the Magicks that I have found, based only on published material, is that Chaos Magick focuses its attention on the individual practitioner, while Maat Magick begins with the individual but extends its concerns to the human race and beyond. To the concept of Chaos Magick's focus on the individual, Mr. Max responds:

"True enough on the surface. My experience is that each Chaos Mage finds their own particular emphasis on the 'beyond' but such focus is not 'canonical' so to speak. In my own case, I see the 'greater' effect of my magical practice as bringing forth the Pandaemoneon - the Aeon of Chaos, the new magical age. Such things as artificially enhanced ESP and mind/machine interfaces may be just around the corner, blurring the line between technology and magic (which is already blurred - tell me the computer isn't a magical device!) To me this is the hope and dream of humanity, and our ultimate salvation."

I see the rise of Chaos Magick as a good sign that Magick is alive and thriving at the close of the Twentieth Century and in the opening years of the Twenty-first. It appears to me that it is heading in the same direction that Maat Magick is, toward an 'Omega Point' of radical individual and species transformation. I anticipate the rise of other Magicks as well, springing from the creativity of those who understand the underlying principles of individuals effecting macrocosmic change by the precision and

aptness of their microcosmic Work.

If you are interested in how that process works, I advise you to obtain and read the following books:

Carroll, Peter J.: *Liber Null and Psychonaut.* Samuel Weiser, York Beach, ME 1987. *Liber Kaos.* Samuel Weiser, York Beach, ME 1993.

Fries, Jan: *Visual Magick: a Manual of Freestyle Shamanism.* Mandrake of Oxford, 1992.

Grant, Kenneth: *Cults of the Shadow.* Frederick Muller Ltd, London 1975. Skoob Books Publishing, London 1993.

Hine, Phil: *Condensed Chaos: An Introduction to Chaos Magic.* New Falcon Publications, Tempe, AZ 1995.

Nema: *Maat Magick: A Guide to Self-Initiation.* Samuel Weiser, York Beach, ME, 1995.

Also see: Horus Maat Lodge: horusmaat.com

Magick for Fools

Lord, what fools these mortals be.

–A Midsummer Night's Dream

When I was a child, my father brought home a marvelous, battery-operated toy called the Mystery Box. It was a black box with a switch marked "ON" and "OFF"; next to the switch was a covered opening. When the switch was moved to "ON", the cover withdrew from the opening, and a little hand emerged. The hand pushed the switch to "OFF", slid back into the opening, and the cover closed over it.

This is an apt, though simplified, metaphor for Magick. It's equally as true to say "Malkuth resolves into Kether again, but after a different manner" as it is to say "Kether resolves into Malkuth again, but after a different manner". Does this mean that the Path of Initiation is a closed circle, delivering you back to your doorstep after a series of fantastic adventures and dire perils? No and yes.

If you rotate your view ninety degrees, you'll see that what appeared to be a circle is actually a spiral, passing through familiar countryside a few miles down the road from your last encounter with the terrain. This often manifests as a sense of déjà vu in trying circumstances, in meeting new acquaintances or in enduring serious Ordeals. Multiple encounters with the same problem mean simply that not all lessons are learned at the

same time, and that wisdom arrives through experiences as well as through revelation.

Neophytes often assume that Initiation proceeds by a linear, though often crooked, path. The experience of walking (and leaping along) that path, however, reveals that each Sphere is revisited repeatedly, each time with a little more intelligence applied to the appreciation of its essence, its virtues and its pitfalls. The same repetition applies to "Crossing the Abyss".

The world of Assiah, the material world and its concerns, has so much gravity and elasticity that it resumes its former shape and immediacy after any number of experiences that proves its illusory nature. Our physical bodies are an essential part of ourselves, and serve to convince us that their surroundings act on them and are acted upon by them. This doesn't mean that matter is evil and spirit is good, despite the centuries in which this philosophy has held sway. What it does mean is that in working Magick, the Initiate must take into account certain inconvenient truths about our engineering, our molecular and atomic makeup, and the impulses encoded into our bodies and influencing our minds.

Many, if not all, Initiates began their pursuit of the High Art with an act of opening the mind to new possibilities. This opening process can be inspired by boredom, desperation, curiosity, rebellion, admiration of a practitioner, or other conditions. If you're ready for Magick, any specific motive to investigate it soon changes to fascination with it. I remember my own early experiences in Magick, the awe and wonder of learning about the transphysical planes, and then actually venturing into the realm of visions, lucid dreaming, and astral expeditions.

I also remember that my initial ideas about what I was experiencing were somewhat askew due to a lack of sufficient data and a lack of understanding of the larger context of transphysical reality. Images and notions from popular culture, images of witches and wizards, gods and demons, miracles and marvels, had to be reinterpreted and comprehended anew.

When revised understandings began to manifest, I was tempted to explain away a lot of things as being "just a psychological phenomenon" or "just telepathic connection", positing states read about, but as yet unattained, as mysterious, alien goals to reach.

A sound way of preparing a generation of students to understand more easily Magick and all of its doings would be to teach poetry as a second language. Literalism is doomed to be mired in paradox, impossibility and experiential refutation. If the Bible, both Old and New Testament, were to be read as literature and poetry instead of as a spiritual textbook and historical record, attempts at institutional indoctrination would be futile, and the mind-rot of fundamentalism would be cured.

If a fool persist in his folly, he would become wise.
— William Blake

Magick demands a new way of seeing, a new point of view. Conventional reality, as presented in school, church, politics and the news media, is a confused patchwork of guesswork, surmise, and uninformed conclusion. Conventional wisdom, that body of opinion and proverbs that the uninitiated swear by (and often at), would hold a Magician to be a fool. How can ritualistic mumbo-jumbo, divination and healing possibly work?

A Neophyte quickly learns the value of silence in the company of the uninitiated. Only experience in the realms traditionally assigned to myth, legend, and fiction can testify to the truth and reality of Magick. Those without such experience will scoff at astral adventures and laugh at the functions of talismans. Until the inexperienced are treated to a personal demonstration by their Holy Guardian Angel, there's no chance for constructive conversation with them. Magickians tend to seek out each other's company because of a shared vision and shared experiences, with individualized details.

Remember your first ritual you performed on the physical

plane. Didn't you feel like a complete fool? I know that I did, and I recall the effort that it took to proceed with the words, the gestures, and mustering of sincerity and concentration. Even with extensive reading in preparation for ritual action, I was nervous about embarrassing myself in the actual doing of it. Of course, there isn't anything embarrassing about doing ritual, but it takes the courage of a fool to begin.

During the early phase of practice, a new opportunity for foolhood opens. In my readings of the words of Teresa of Avila and John of the Cross, friends and mystics in Medieval Spain, I encountered descriptions of my own experiences in Magick. There's a period of "sweetness" – a honeymoon, if you will – that encourages a person to keep pursuing his or her chosen path. For Christian mystics, it brings visions and a sense of the presence of God. For me, and for various Magickal colleagues, it took the form of a coin appearing out of thin air, a sofa moving a few feet during a shared astral working, a potted aloe plant moving sideways from the top of my refrigerator and crashing to the floor, etc. Minor PSI phenomena like those described above, uncanny "coincidences", significant numbers presenting themselves on car registration plates or on television, all contribute to the conviction that "there must be something to this Magick business". If you take it as a confirmation that you're going in the right direction—and if you continue along in that direction—then the odd events have served their proper purpose.

If, on the other hand, you become enamored of these epiphenomena, and mistake them for the results of your Workings, you might be inclined to pursue them. This doesn't work for long, and you become the wrong kind of fool, a mere prestidigitator of manifestations. Other than possibly impressing your friends, there's little point in being able to know who's about to call you on the phone or in being able to conjure up a change of weather.

A chela called out to his guru from the far side of the

river, "Watch me, master." He drew his consciousness into his Manipura Chakra, slowed his breathing, and walked across the water to join his guru on the near shore.

"It's taken me seven years of meditation and purification by austerities and much spiritual work to be able to do this," he said. "Surely it means I'm nearing enlightenment!"

The guru shook his head sadly and asked, "My son, why did you not take the ferry-boat?"

The main problem with becoming attached to Magickal epiphenomena and the awe and wonder they produce is that the honeymoon is soon over—in Magick and Mysticism, as well as in romance.

After the sweetness comes the dryness. You notice that the incidence of the little miracles begins to fall. You barely feel the rush of power during ritual, and the astral realms may close themselves to you. No longer do you experience spontaneous visions, or the sense of impending events, or even the bothersome "astral chill". Even more distressing, you begin to feel tired when it's time to do ritual, meditation, yoga, katas, or whatever your chosen practices have been. You feel the urge to make excuses for postponing or omitting them altogether.

The deep, solid core of Will is the only thing that keeps you going. This is similar to, if not identical with, the quality that religious people call faith, but it is based on experience rather than on belief.

If you're not enjoying the rewards of your actions, isn't it foolish to keep on performing them? Indeed it is, and it's in this period that many cease active ritual practice, or stop their meditating. Some revert to armchair Magick, preening themselves on their knowledge without working to apply it.

Others search out other paths and abandon Magick entirely. It takes a true fool to continue in tedium, boredom and frustration, not to mention the lack of spiritual consolation and sense of isolation from all forms of the Divine Intelligence, other than your own.

Persistence pays off, however, and the period of dryness opens into a deeper, subtler understanding of yourself and others, and of how Magick works.

For fools rush in where angels fear to tread. – Alexander Pope.

A prime opportunity for foolishness to manifest is in the quest for the Knowledge and Conversation of the Holy Guardian Angel, that landmark event in your course of Initiation. You've learned that there is a superior, benevolent entity who longs for conscious contact with you, an entity able to illuminate your True Will, to be your intimate mentor, to guide your actions and Initiations. You begin daily invocations of your Angel, invocations that feed your desire for the encounter, that generate a longing for union with this marvelous being.

If you retain a habit of literalism in your pursuit of the Angel, you won't be able to recognize your encounters with it when they happen. It's the wrong kind of folly in this case to have a mental image of the Angel as you think it will appear. Not only will such an image blind you to genuine meetings with your Angel, but it will also provide a template for astral counterfeits of the angel generated by entities seeking access to your lifeforce.

An open mind backed by caution is the right kind of folly. Whatever presents itself should be verified in as many ways as you can think of. Materialists and atheists would call you a fool for entertaining a belief in something you've not yet encountered, but your Angel provides preliminary verification of its reality by the void you feel without it.

The attainment of the Knowledge and Conversation of the Holy Guardian Angel is necessary to establish the beacon of True Will that illuminates the cluster of choices we face every day. Without it, we're practicing the wrong kind of foolishness, acting from custom, habit, impulse and other people's opinions. Without this Knowledge and Conversation with the Angel, we "rush in" to situations that can, and often do, divert us from

the course of True Will and from the fulfillment of our life's purpose.

A fool and his money are soon parted. - Proverb

Perhaps the most significant opportunity for Magickal folly lurks on the brink of the Abyss. If we take "money" as the symbol and talisman for all we value, covet, and hold dear, the parting from it comes scarcely soon enough. The Abyss requires a blind leap, as it were, with no assurance that there's another side to it. On the familiar side is everything you've worked for, achieved, concluded, attained and accomplished, and all of this must be left behind.

It's one of the few clear choices in life. Either the world as that which we were born into, with all its physics, characters and quirks, is the "real" world, or it is a phantasm, an illusion, a dream. The world includes not only all physical manifestation, but also all ideas, words, art, feelings, relationships, knowledge, and convictions.

Leaping the Abyss is like the shadow of martyrdom. The martyr dies gladly in anticipation of the rewards of the afterlife. Who dares the Abyss has no such hope, for the afterlife is as illusory as this present life. Martyrdom identifies the self with the physical body, since that is what is relinquished in an act misnamed self-sacrifice. The leaping fool relinquishes everything, in a giant spiritual potlatch* that bestows upon him or her the ultimate freedom, even though flesh-life continues—but after a different manner.

What becomes of what the fool gives up on the edge of the Abyss? Who inherits the fruits of experience, the memories of a lifetime, the Initiations and attainments? Specific methodology and results, insights and discoveries can be had from a well-kept Magickal Record, but the deeds and states themselves are

* Ceremony of Pacific Northwest tribes of Native Americans where all possessions are given away with ritual intent.

absorbed by the Magickal Current and circulated for the benefit of those who attune themselves to the Current.

In the abandonment of all possessions, the leaping fool also sacrifices him- or her-self, surrendering to the Void, becoming a non-person, dissolving into the flow of things. These words are only a descriptive approximation, since the "leap" is more of a recognition of eternal non-entity than it is of anything else. Even the subtlest realization in the course of self-knowledge is a part of the dream from which one awakens to the inexpressible fact of no-thing-ness.

Total surrender is not an easy thing to accomplish; there seems to be a recurring "last drop" remaining after each scouring, a tiny, piping gnat affirming its continuity. The holy fool persists in disowning things; the damned fool is often trapped in the pride of his or her renunciation. The leap occurs when you give up trying to give up. About the only true thing that can be said about crossing the Abyss is that it renders physical death an anticlimax.

The Magickal Current/Tao/Maat of change begins to run your life then, making conscious decisions unnecessary. If you're gone, what's left to do or to observe anything? Your bodies (physical, astral, etheric, spiritual, etc.) assume that normality prevails, and they go about their business as usual, only more calmly and harmoniously.

Here, then, is the post-Abyss fool: life goes on, apparently as usual, and yet anxiety is missing. Not much bothers this fool, since she or he sees that all events are both illusory and perfect. There is no longer a True Will to do, since True Will is the Tao, the Magickal Currrent, the Maat of change, and it is the "doer" in all evens. All of the study, ritual, Ordeals, time and hard work put into the pursuit of Magick has left a worthy vessel in the service of Tao. Specific events are of no consequence.

So it is that all true Magick is Magick for fools, and all false "Magick" is Magick for damned fools. It's a fundamental aphorism of Maat Magick that "All valid systems of Initiation

self-destruct upon successful completion." Organizations that grow around an interest in the High Art can be useful in that they can preserve Magickal Records and the forms of effective rituals, but in most cases the organizations harden into institutions that serve the base interests of Ego and spiritual price.

The holy fool is free to enjoy the greatest show on earth (or the only game in town), with no worry as to how it all turns out. Austin Osman Spare puts it very nicely in his formula of "Does not matter, need not be." Aleister Crowley does likewise in the Vision of No Difference.

It's our brave but doomed little self that moves the switch to "ON" on the Mystery Box of Magick when we first begin our study and practice. This act contains within itself its own opposite state of "OFF", both for the Mystery Box and for its operator.

First published in 1996 in STARFIRE Volume II, Number 1.
Starfire Publishing Ltd., BCM Starfire, London WC1N 3XX, U.K.

MAGICKAL HEALING IN THEORY AND PRACTICE

Bodies Balanced in Health

(A workshop presentation)

Introduction

I'm glad that you're here. My name is Maggie Ingalls, and I'm also known as Nema. I've written a book called *Maat Magick: a Guide to Self-Initiation*, plus a few others. I'm a high priestess and Elder in the Circle of the Sacred Grove, Church of Pantheist Wicca. I've been a member of Kenneth Grant's Typhonian Order under the name Andahadna, and I'm currently an Adi Nath tantra yogini under the name Padme Devi. I'm a founding member of the Horus Maat Lodge, online at horusmaat.com.

I've never been attracted to the practice of medicine as an art or a science, but on various occasions I've been asked to help people in pain, discomfort or illness. The knowledge and the experiences that it came from might be useful for other people to have. I've gathered much of what I know for you.

Some things came from my mother, grandmothers, aunties and friends. Some things came from science classes and the Boy Scouts field manuals. Wise elders have taught me much about watching and listening. Other practices were learned from

inspired experimentation, and still others arrived in the white-hot rush of unlearned knowledge. I only recommend to others what I have tried myself.

I see our bodies in the plural. In many practical situations, it's logical to refer to our physical body, emotional body, astral body, social body, etc. in describing a human situation or condition. The idea of several bodies (or souls, depending on your point of view) is part metaphor and part prosaic description.

Thanks in advance for your patience with words.

Bring Out Your Dead

Our physical body developed an immune system to protect us from invaders whose effects, whether chemical, mechanical, parasitical or otherwise, could harm us or kill us.

The physical body, in and with its parts, can knit broken bones, fill wounds with scar tissue, close gashes in skin, stop bleeding with clotting, scab over skinned knees and perform countless other ordinary miracles. Much of medicine consists of cleaning up wounds, realigning bones, and controlling invaders through radiation, chemistry, and other means.

Whether we're dealing with a disease, injury, imbalance or general malaise, or whether we're practicing preventive hygiene, we can assist ourselves through Magick, common sense, intuition and will.

Recycling

Begin with your practical perimeter, be it your yard, house, apartment, mobile home, bedroom, dorm, or cell. Clean up all clutter, file or store what's useful, remove what's not. Your physical body, as well as your transphysical bodies, will respond well to improved cleanliness and order in a relaxed atmosphere.

Don't pitch away that which might be useful to others,

or what can be 'officially' recycled in your area. Separate your newspapers from your office, school paper, and mail, from your slick paper and magazines. Save your clear glass and brown glass, separate your steel cans from the aluminum. If your local government doesn't collect, take your material to a recycling center.

Sort your clothes between those which are in good condition, are your current size and wearable, and that you still like. From the reject pile, sort those clothes which aren't in good enough shape for a person to wear from those which are. Donate the latter to a resale organization (like Volunteers of America, Salvation Army, etc.) and turn the unwearables into rags, quilt patches, and craft project materials.

You'll probably begin to feel lighter and more at ease at this point, but keep going. It gets better.

When we consider our books, another level of consciousness participates in the decisions we make about their disposal. In the current age of technology, the idea of 'book' has been extended to include photographs, films, tapes, discs, programs, files, codes, and beyond. Perhaps book now means any object, device, or process that preserves information over time with minimal distortion.

When the time is right, review your books. Keep those you love and/or need. If there are books that should leave your possession, try to find an appropriate home for each. The same applies to magazines and musical recordings. Be sure not to pressure anyone into taking what you're offering. If you find organizations that share your interests, donate the gently-used books. See if nursing homes and assisted-living institutions are accepting such donations. To make life easy for the books you keep, choose the filing system(s) that you like, and arrange your books accordingly.

Letting go of Magickal tools, talismans, and outgrown ritual objects can be a difficult process, since we form a bond with them even stronger than the ones we have with our books. Two

ideas can help in this process: 1) a mage has the ownership of nothing and the use of everything and 2) a faithful servant deserves its rest.

Humans are toolmakers. Tools extend our powers and abilities, and so we come to trust and even love them. Humans are also slave-takers and servant-makers. Many current civilizations no longer practice legal slavery, but some individuals still try to control others through force and fear.

In some older styles of Magick, the mage was expected to summon and command elemental spirits and demons to carry out his or her will. In some contemporary systems, notably in Chaos Magick, servitors are constructed to carry out repeated or extended tasks to relieve the mage from the tedium of maintaining personal attention on them. In the spirit of simplicity and minimalism, question what you actually need among your possessions.

The wiser you become in the ability to cause change, the less you need servants. The closer you work to the physical Kingdom, the more important your tools become. Working in the Kingdom takes time and effort, but it provides psycho-spiritual exercise for the benefit of your knowledge and understanding. Some tools lose their effectiveness for a Mage when understanding expands and deepens through experience. Sorting through your Magickal possessions (perhaps a contradiction in terms) is a more complex action than deciding the fate of your mundane troves of things.

We sometimes find ourselves in a teaching situation, so I think it's wise to keep a set of tools/weapons for instruction by demonstration. There are also times when the sight and the feel of familiar tools enhances one's own sense of connection with the Magickal Current.

(Note: Familiars and such enjoy an elemental form of consciousness and continuity. They served you, now, if their time is done, it may be best to release them to the Elysian Fields rather than relegate them to some astral Glue Factory. - Nema)

The tools we use are usually beautiful things: painted or carved images, incense burners, crystals, chalices and blades, wands and staves. I find the best way to dispose of them it give them away to people who need and will use them. It's wise and ethical first to remove your personal and intentional energies from the tool or sacred tchochke (Never call up what you can't put down.).

The second best way of disposal is to feed them to the elements, each according to its nature: incineration, dissolution, dispersal and burial, alone and in combination.

Banishing Toxins

Once you have the number of your possessions reduced and arranged or stored to your liking, it's good to clear your atmosphere (or "atma-sphere") with banishings. Dramatic events, positive or negative, often leave traces of themselves within us and within our surroundings. The ghosts of events are just one source of astral trash. We generate most of our own trash by resentment, brooding, disrespect (given or received), becoming fixated or obsessed on someone or something, etc.

Whether we're being called upon to help someone else or to help ourselves, we need to be at our best in order to do our will. By performing our Magick on ourselves first, we find out, in general, how the procedure works on us. If our colleagues agree to try the rite, charm or spell and then discuss it with us, we have more experience of it available among us, to everyone's benefit.

Use the banishing rite(s) you know and trust, or use a short series of them, beginning with your surroundings and ending at your spiritual core. These can be used for yourself or for other people up to the astral level. For astral and above, stand facing the client, rub your hands warm. Position both hands about six inches above his/her head, and bring them down slowly on

either side. Touch your hands to the ground then shake off the energies. Repeat this three times.

Move to stand facing the client's left side, your hands above his/her head, then draw down your hands to touch the ground three times, again shaking free the energies each time.

End by holding your left hand above his/her head, with your right hand above the coccyx/tailbone. Draw power deeply from below the soles of your feet, then move your right hand slowly up the client's spine. Touch your hands briefly above the client's head, then open them quickly, releasing and boosting any rough energies skyward. Pause for three heartbeats, then clap your hands sharply above the client's head, and stand back.

Curing Nightmares

When my granddaughter Gwyneth was a young girl, she shared with me a technique that she had discovered to rid herself of nightmares: she'd banish her bed. We didn't go into the technical details, but I thought the concept made good sense. In addition to imposing order on the emotional levels of her life, an order that she defined and enforced, Gwyn was learning about the nature of Magick and about her own nature.

Of a similar approach is the use of dreamcatchers.

I believe that it's good to teach children Magick, if those children are yours. For all kinds of legal and emotional reasons, make sure that the seekers who find you are legally adults.

Parasites / Psychic Vampires, Leeches

People can drain each other's energy and vitality without consciously intending to do so. People also can have an unrecognized draining effect by demanding (and getting) more than their fair share of your time and attention.

The more innocent ones might say that they feel so much

better after talking to you, that you're a great listener, and a really good friend. The less innocent can use your vulnerability and kindness as a means of control, dominance and abuse. There are also lower-astral entities and some 'gateway locations' that can affect your energy-levels, mental clarity and emotional balance.

Sometimes a vampiric situation can be solved by leaving the presence of the vampire, but circumstances can prevent this simple solution. If you're dealing with an employer, supervisor, manager, co-worker, spouse or family member, you may need to resort to closing your aura to them.

I recommend the writings of Dion Fortune, (Violet Firth) particularly her *Psychic Self-Defense.*

In it, she describes how she dealt with a vampiric employer, an older woman who had verbally abused and harassed her. When seated in the vampire's presence, Dion would interlace her fingers, her hands in her lap and her feet together, flat on the floor. Then she would envision her aura as a diamond-hard shell around her, a shell that Dion could penetrate at will but was impenetrable from the outside. Her persecutor complained that Dion was cold and distant from her. I believe Dion just smiled.

It's generally good to help other people when possible, but not every request is genuine. Find ways to hone your truth-detection powers and learn how to smell a rat. Compassion doesn't mean gullibility.

Hauntings & Astral Chills

Buildings, places, vehicles, machines and appliances can be haunted by energies from past events and people. In addition to the banishing process mentioned before, it can help to Magickally charge the water you use to mop the floor, and to charge the vinegar, ammonia or commercial product you use to clean windows and other glass surfaces. Traditional protections include placing a clove of garlic on top of door lintels and

window frames. Scattering salt around a room purifies it, as does burning sweetgrass and fanning out the smoke with a feather.

The scent of herbs that have been Magickally charged can contribute to the well-being of people and places through baths, sachets, and pillows. There are a number of herbal books on the market, and herb gardens can thrive in small places.

Dream pillows feature mugwort, wormwood sachets banish lower-astral parasites. The scent of lavender, hyssop and sage flowers calm anxieties and worry. Catnip, lemon balm and chamomile teas can tone and soothe the digestive system. Some edible flowers, like borage, honeysuckle, nasturtiums and honey locust seem to elevate perceptions and mood.

Not everything that grows in a garden is good to eat, however. Eating rhubarb leaves, or any part of a castor bean plant, can be deadly. It's a good idea to research unfamiliar plants before tasting them.

Magickal Techniques Beyond Banishing

Talismans: Caduceus & Tarot cards

Traditionally, talismans are pictures of words, numbers, shapes and patterns which express the mage's desire. The Seal of Solomon is a classic talisman. The healing talisman that came to me in a family medical situation has been helpful to me over the years.

On a black background is an orange octagon. On the octagon is a green staff with a yellow/gold sphere of the sun as its head. Right below the sphere is a spread pair of wings, horizontally layered green and yellow/gold. A white snake with a black eye and a black snake with a white eye are entwined up the staff. This is the Caduceus, staff of Hermes or Mercury, god of the healing arts, messenger of the gods, teacher of science and

communication.

The serpents stand for the duality of the physical world, for the creativity of the Yin and Yang, for balance of Tao and Teh. Orange is the Queen scale color of Hod, or Splendor, on the Tree of Life. On that same scale, black is the color of Binah on the ToL. Binah is Understanding, linked to Saturn, to the Mother Ocean, to the City of the Pyramids.

My sister-in-law, Mary, had returned to Cincinnati from the Navy base in the Pacific where she lived with my brother, Jim. The Navy doctors had told her that she had cancer, and had suggested she consult with stateside civilian specialists. When I found her, she was in the 4th floor 'terminal' ward (or so the nurse termed it) at a local hospital.

We hugged and cried and talked for a while, then I described the caduceus to her. While she pictured it, I poured healing energy into her for as long as I could. Several days later, when free time turned up in a world of small kids, I decided to visit Mary again.

I was astounded and pleased to see her walking on the sidewalk in the hospital's neighborhood. When I asked her what happened, she said that her doctors told her that she'd been misdiagnosed, and that she had no cancer. Right.

Unfortunately, I've lost touch with Mary since her divorce from Jim. He remarried and now has grandchildren with his second wife, Rose, and their two sons.

What can I claim for the talisman? Through the years since its application to Mary, it continues to be helpful in healing people. Does a person have to believe in its powers for those powers to work? I don't think so, but you need to pay attention to your bodies, and to those of your client, in order to understand what they need to be well and balanced.

Tarot cards often make effective talismans for a number of purposes, that of healing among them. I'm most familiar with the Thoth deck, and you should use your favorite pack design for your Tarot talisman.

What are the best cards to use for healing? Begin with the four eights of Wands, Cups, Swords (or Blades), and Disks (or Pentacles). Eight is attributed to Hermes, Mercury, Thoth, Hanuman, Messengers and healing gods. Sometimes symptoms can be linked with the traditional elements as: wands = fire/fever; cups = water/sweating/chills/thirst; blades = air/breathing obstructions/ coughing/ sneezing/ asthma; discs or pentacles = earth/ bones/ skeleton/ arthritis/ nerve or muscle problems.

A more detailed choice can be made with a few columns from *Liber 777*, A. Crowley:

#	Body Part(s)	Tarot Card	Signs, etc.
0	Respiratory system	The Fool	Air
1	Brain, nerves	The Magus	Mercury
2	Lymph system	High Priestess	Moon
3	Genital system	Empress	Venus
4	Head & face	The Star	Aries
5	Shoulders & arms	Hierophant	Taurus
6	Lungs	Lovers	Gemini
7	Stomach	Chariot	Cancer
8	Heart	Hermit	Leo
9	The back	Wheel of Fortune	Virgo
10	Digestive system	Justice	Jupiter
11	Liver	Hanged Man	Water
12	Organs of Nutrition	Death	Scorpio
13	Intestines	Temperance	Venus

14	Hips & thighs	The Devil	Sagittarius
15	Genital system	Tower	Capricorn
16	Muscular system	Emperor	Mars
17	Kidneys & bladder	The Moon	Aquarius
18	Legs & feet	The Sun	Pisces
19	Circulatory system	The Aeon	Sun
20	Organs of Circulation	The Universe	Fire
21	Excretory system		Saturn
22	Skeleton		Earth
23	Organs of Intelligence		Spirit

Sigils: A.O. Spare's Method

Sigils are abstract shapes constructed from the letters of words of desire. The shapes are, in a sense, "shaped charges" of powered will shot into the cosmos on the force of intense experience. The destruction of the sigil often marks the release of manifestation.

The forces operating sigils are powerful but simple. They generally don't recognize the word "no", or similar negations, so your expression of Will should be put in positive terms. Rather than write "I want to stop smoking", phrase it as "I want clean lungs." Rather than write "Remove my back pain", put it as "I want a healthy back."

It seems the theory is, with sigils, "to mention is to invoke." So with some inventive "slight of mind" (a Chaos Magick term), you can manifest your desire(s) with a minimum of unintended consequences. You can construct a sigil for yourself and/or for other people.

For example, for upcoming cataract surgery, I could write

"I want clear eyes". I would then strike through ever duplicated letter to get "I w a n t c l e r y s". Next, I combine the letters with each other, sharing parts with each other, backward, rotated, upside down, within, surrounding, etc., until the original sentence can't be discerned in the resulting design.

This design, or sigil, can be copied onto other objects and material, depending on your choice of a method of destruction/disposal. One of my favorite ways is to eat the sigil, so rice paper for hand-rolling cigarettes is useful. Pencil 'lead' is really graphite and clay, nontoxic as far as I know. If you have the patience, you could use food coloring and toothpicks to scribe on the rice paper. In the process of transcribing the sigil, you're charging it through your work and your intention, but you can charge it further through drumming, dancing, chanting, and other means.

The sigil is then turned upside down and forgotten. This is the key part of sigil work: the forgetting. It's best done by getting busy with other concerns and distractions.

The next time you experience strong feelings from passion or pain, anger, despair, awe or orgasm, recall the sigil to your consciousness and blow it away into everything and nothing. The physical sigil can be eaten, or given to the elements as you see fit.

Invocations for Prayer and Administration

Some mages work with godforms and others don't. Some of those who work with godforms do so in literal belief, others see a god or gods as metaphors for principles or qualities. Earlier in my history of Initiation (before email and the Internet), I wrote to Kenneth Grant to ask him if the gods were real. He answered "The gods are as real as we are—but how real are we?"

If you involve deities in a healing, there are two major

approaches that I know of: invocation of the god as an invitation to use the mage's body and faculties to do therapeutic actions for the client (drumming, dancing, chanting, etc.) or invocation of the god's presence as supplicant, asking the god to heal the client as a being separate from the mage.

Which approach you use depends on your understanding of how things work in the realms of Magick and in the realms of physical reality.

Where does it hurt?
Talk to your parts—and listen.

- mantra meditation

- pranayam

- seider & smiling into your stomach (per Jan Fries)

Go to a pro, research the system.

- online medical websites

- community/NGO clinics

- personal referrals

Other Publications by
Black Moon Publishing

The Faces of Babalon
A Compilation of Women's Voices by Mishlen Linden,
Linda Falorio, Soror Chen, Nema and Raven Greywalker

Waters of Return
The Aeonic Flow of Voudoo by Louis Martinié

A Priest's Head, A Drummer's Hands
New Orleans Voodoo Order of Service by Louis Martinié

The Priesthood
Parameters and Responsibilities by Nema

Maatian Meditations and Considerations
A Continuation of Past Writings on "She Who Moves"
by Nema

The Compleat Liber Pennae Praenumbra
by Nema

The Horus Maat Lodge: The Grimoire of a PanAeonic Tribe
by The Inner Council of the HML

Enochian Temples
by Benjamin Rowe

The Book of the Seniors
by Benjamin Rowe

The 91 Parts of the Earth
by Benjamin Rowe

BLACKMOONPUBLISHING.COM

CPSIA information can be obtained
at www.ICGtesting.com
Printed in the USA
LVHW091504180520
655935LV00002B/660